Educational Politics

Pressure groups and faith-based schools

GEOFFREY WALFORD
Department of Educational Studies
University of Oxford

Avebury

Aldershot • Brookfield USA • Hong Kong • Singapore • Sydney

Published by
Avebury
Ashgate Publishing Limited
Gower House
Croft Road
Aldershot
Hants GU11 3HR
England

Ashgate Publishing Company
Old Post Road
Brookfield
Vermont 05036
USA

British Library Cataloguing in Publication Data

Walford, Geoffrey
    Educational Politics: Pressure Groups and
    Faith-based Schools
    I. Title
    377.0941
ISBN 1 85628 907 9

Library of Congress Catalog Card Number: 95-81137

Printed and bound by Athenaeum Press, Ltd.,
Gateshead, Tyne & Wear.

Contents

Acknowledgements

Empirically based educational research is far from being a solitary activity. It is only possible because of the help and support given by colleagues, institutions, gatekeepers and those whose activities are the subject of the research.

I have been particularly fortunate in the support that I have been given by all of these groups. At Aston Business School, Henry Miller gave his usual encouragement and firm collegiality, while the Social Innovation research Group provided part of the necessary funding. The Nuffield Foundation was also kind enough to give me one of their Small Grants from 1992-1994, without which most of the interviews and visits would not have been possible. Since my move to Oxford University I have benefited from a similarly sympathetic and supportive research culture that has enabled me to complete this work only a little behind schedule. I am also indebted to Colin Poyntz for the enthusiasm and care with which he assisted me in undertaking the survey part of the study.

I acknowledge with thanks the publishers of some of my previous articles and book chapters for allowing me to reuse sections from those publications within this book. While there is much that is new and previously unpublished in this account, it also draws upon these earlier published works and forms a new mosaic from the fragments. Chapter two is a revised and extended version of Colin Poyntz and Geoffrey Walford (1994) 'The new Christian schools: A survey' *Educational Studies*, 20, 1, pp. 127-143, and incorporates a short section from Geoffrey Walford (1994) 'Weak choice, strong choice and the new Christian schools' in J. Mark Halstead (ed.) *Parental Choice and Education: Principles, policies and practice*, London, Kogan Page, pp. 139-150. Chapter four includes some material from Geoffrey Walford (1991) 'The reluctant private sector: of small schools, people and politics' in Geoffrey Walford (ed.) *Private Schooling: tradition, change and diversity*, London Paul Chapman, pp. 115-32. Chapter six uses sections from Geoffrey Walford (1995) 'The Northbourne amendments: Is the House of Lords a garbage can?' *Journal of Education Policy* 10 (4). Chapter eight draws upon Geoffrey Walford (1995) 'The Christian Schools Campaign - a successful educational pressure group?' *British Educational Research Journal* 21 (4), and chapter ten contains sections from Geoffrey Walford (1994) 'The new religious grant-maintained schools' *Education Management and Administration* 22, 2, pp. 123-130.

1 Introduction

The 1993 Education Act can be seen as a victory. Various sections of the Act can be seen to have been directly influenced by a particular educational pressure group, and the objectives of that group were to a large extent achieved in that legislation. The pressure group was the Christian Schools Campaign and the particular legislation concerned the right for various sponsor groups to apply to the Secretary of State for Education to establish new forms of grant-maintained school. This book examines the schools that supported the pressure group, the activities of that pressure group and the implications of the policy change.

The 1993 Education Act is a long and complex piece of legislation. Among other changes, it enabled the establishment of the Funding Agency for Schools in England and the Schools Funding Council for Wales, made it easier for local education authority and voluntary schools to become grant-maintained, amended legislation on special educational needs, and gave powers to the Secretaries of State to deal with schools deemed to be failing. All these changes are of major significance, but the Act also gave new powers to the Secretaries of State and the new Funding Agencies for Schools that eventually may lead to a thoroughgoing reconceptualization of the way in which state-maintained schooling is provided in England and Wales.

The Secretaries of State were given powers to establish new grant-maintained school in two different ways. The first simply deals with cases where the Funding Agencies see the need for a new school due to changes in population or similar circumstances, but the second allows independent sponsors to propose the establishment of new schools. Through this second procedure, if the Secretary of State approves individual proposals, the way is open for England and Wales

1

to have state-funded schools that have the aim of fostering, for example, Muslim, Buddhist, or evangelical Christian beliefs or which wish to promote particular educational philosophies. Existing faith-based private schools are now able to apply to become reestablished as grant-maintained schools. In the long term, this change may be the most significant result of the 1993 Education Act, for it further blurs the boundary between private and public provision, encourages significant private financial investment in schools, and shifts some of the responsibility for provision to local, private initiative.

Technically, it was already possible for LEAs to support various religiously-based schools through voluntary aided status. At present about 28 per cent of primary aged pupils and 17 per cent of secondary pupils are in voluntary schools. Some 16 per cent of schools in England are voluntary aided, with a further 11 per cent being voluntary controlled or special agreement schools. The vast majority of these voluntary schools are Church of England or Roman Catholic schools, and there are a very few Methodist and Jewish schools. Although several existing Muslim and evangelical Christian private schools have applied to their LEAs to become voluntary aided, all such requests have so far been rejected. Usually this has happened at the LEA level, but occasionally the LEA has agreed, while central government has refused the request. This was the case in the well-publicised example of Islamia primary school where Brent local education authority supported the application for voluntary aided status but it was turned down by the Department for Education in August 1993. The 1993 Act removes any barriers to the support of faith-based schools erected by local authorities, and passes the decision directly to the Department for Education. Ministers have indicated that 'denominational need' will play a significant part in the consideration of proposals for sponsored grant-maintained schools, and that over-supply of places in nearby schools (as traditionally defined within two or three mile limits) will not necessarily lead to rejection of proposals.

These new grant-maintained schools will differ from existing grant-maintained schools in that sponsors will have to pay for at least 15 per cent of costs relating to the provision of a site for the school and/or school buildings. In return for this financial contribution, through the school's trust deeds and instruments of government, the sponsors will be able to ensure that the school retains its original purpose. In particular, restrictions on making a 'significant change in the religious character' of these grant-maintained schools are explicitly built into the Act. Additionally, the composition of the governing body allows the sponsors to ensure that the religious objectives of the school are maintained and that the religious beliefs and practices of teaching staff are taken into consideration in appointments. Where an existing private school becomes grant-maintained, teachers will not be automatically bound to the School Teachers' Pay and Conditions Act 1991. The schools will, of course, have to teach the National Curriculum, but special arrangements for the teaching of religious education can be detailed in the trust deeds, and different arrangements can be made about the character of collective religious worship. The admissions process can give preference to children from families with particular beliefs in the same way as can existing Roman Catholic or Church of England voluntary schools.

The legislation that permits these new faith-based grant-maintained schools was strongly influenced by continued campaigning from an interlocking network of pressure groups that represent a range of 'reluctant' private schools (Walford, 1991). The most prominent groups that have campaigned for such schools are several Muslim pressure groups (including the Islamia Schools Trust and, more recently, the Muslim Parliament) and the Christian Schools Campaign (CSC) which represents about 65 private evangelical Christian schools.

The book as a whole is concerned with the nature and activities of the Christian Schools Campaign, and begins to analyse and assess its influence on education policy. It is based upon a long-term research project that started in 1988 and included an interview and postal survey of the 65 schools with links to the Christian Schools Trust (Poyntz and Walford, 1994), interviews with key politicians and activists involved with the Christian Schools Campaign, attendance and nonparticipant observation at various policy and planning meetings, and the use of documentary data.

Chapter two gives a description of the nature of the schools involved with the Christian Schools Trust and thus having links to the Christian Schools Campaign. It gives a statistical picture of the schools derived from the survey and interviews, examines the special features of the schools and the ideologies that underlie them, and describes some of the diversity that can be found within the group. This is followed by chapter three which examines the theological and pragmatic justifications used by Christians to support separate Christian schools. It then discusses the reasons why the schools were initially established and how this relates to the Campaign.

Chapter four outlines the structure and purpose of the Christian Schools Campaign, and its relationships with other campaigning organizations. It traces the ways in which a prestigious group of sponsors was gathered together to ensure that its ideas and activities were well reported in newspapers. It examines how the Campaign was established, its links to politicians on the New Right, and to particular Members of Parliament and Members of the House of Lord, and the relationships between the Campaign and the actual schools. The initial links with the Prime Minister's Policy Unit are examined.

Of particular importance in the Campaign was a House of Lords debate in March 1991 on a Bill put forward by Baroness Cox who was working with the Christian Schools Trust. This is the subject of chapter five. This Bill, which was written by Stuart Sexton for the Campaign, was designed to make it possible for religious organizations to establish their own grant-maintained schools and to make it easier for such groups to obtain voluntary aided status for existing private schools. This motion was withdrawn after a four-hour debate as there was no chance of it becoming law due to time factors, but the debate received considerable publicity and acted as a focus for the campaign.

The 1992 Education (Schools) Act provided another opportunity for the Christian Schools Campaign to influence policy, and this is discussed in chapter six. On this occasion Lord Northbourne proposed amendments (that had been written by the Christian Schools Campaign working with CARE Campaigns) on inspection and publication of information by schools. These amendments focused on the belief that all schools transmit 'spiritual and moral' values and that these should be clear in information given about schools and inspected by Registered Inspectors. The Lords reacted very favourably towards the amendments, probably because they saw the government's focus on examination results as too narrow, and Baroness Blatch was forced to recognise the feelings of the House and reconsider. She later put forward government amendments that dealt with inspection, but left publication of information to Regulations rather than primary legislation. The government extended the basis for inspection of schools to specifically include 'the spiritual, moral, social and cultural' development of pupils.

Chapter seven examines the demise of the Campaign, looking in particular at theological and practical tensions within and between the new Christian schools and the Campaign itself. This chapter also includes a discussion of the role of Patrons in the Campaign, especially that of the Archbishop of Canterbury.

By late 1992 the aims of the Christian Schools Campaign could be seen as similar to relevant aspects of government policy. The ideology of choice had become so powerful that it had become difficult to deny parents the right to establish their own schools if they wished - they simply added to the diversity of schools that now were seen as a prerequisite for choice. The case for faith-based schools also chimed well with John Patten's (then Secretary of State) religious views. Chapter eight tackles two issues. The first is the way in which the idea of inspecting 'spiritual and moral values' was to be interpreted, and the second concerns the role of Christian activists in influencing the 1993 Education Act. There are some clear examples in this Act of specific changes being made at the behest of those involved with the new Christian schools.

This abbreviated outline of the political Campaign goes some way to explain the importance of the new Christian schools in terms of the development of educational policy. The final two chapters of the book examine the political context in which the pressure group operated in more detail and begin an analysis of its activities. In brief, it is argued that a micropolitical perspective can be used to help understand this particular case study, but that this analysis must be situated within an examination of the wider social and political context. The group was successful in achieving its aims because its agenda meshed with that of several New Right groups. But the situation was complex, and there are several examples of muddle and simple serendipity than need to be acknowledged.

Chapter nine also examines the likelihood of new Christian schools from with the group actually applying for grant-maintained status, while the final chapter places the activities of the pressure group within a wider social context and examines the equity issues associated with the success of the campaign.

2 What are the new Christian schools?

Introduction

The 1992 White Paper on Education took *Choice and Diversity* as its title. It advocated greater differences between schools and provided the base for the increased diversity of schools within the maintained sector, and selection of children for particular schools, that has followed the 1993 Education Act. Such changes may be seen as an integral part of a larger privatization process (Walford, 1990) for they are designed to make the state-maintained system more like the private system, where diversity between schools is a key characteristic.

It may surprise some readers that diversity should be seen as a central feature of the British private sector, for political debate is often conducted as if the private schools were homogeneous and all of uniformly high academic standard. This is far from the case. While the fiercely selective and elitist 'public' schools such as Winchester College or Westminster School clearly provide a highly academic environment for their pupils, there are many other private schools that offer little beyond snob appeal. In such schools a measure of social exclusiveness is achieved by excluding 'less desirable' children whose parents cannot afford high fees.

That the private sector is usually seen as relatively homogeneous is due, in large part, to a concerted effort by most of the schools to present themselves as such. During the late 1960s the major 'public' schools had been severely attacked by the Labour government for their elitism, and the Public Schools Commission had proposed dramatic changes that most would have found highly undesirable. Although a Conservative government was returned in 1970, the schools established the Independent Schools Information Service (ISIS) in 1972 and the Independent Schools Joint Council (ISJC) in 1974 to protect their interests. Both organizations included associations representing a broad range of the well-established private schools. The seven Associations within ISIS and ISJC include the Headmasters Conference, the Girls' Schools Association, and the Incorporated Association of Preparatory Schools and thus represent boys, girls and co-educational schools for all ages. The new organizations officially buried the 'public' school terminology, with its implications of elitism, and the sector as a whole presented itself as 'independent'. As Rae (1981) argues: 'That the term 'public school' should be obsolescent is something of a triumph for the schools' public relations...Few British people could be expected to rally to the defence of the public schools, but independence was a wider and much more fundamental issue.'

By 1995, the 1349 schools represented within ISIS/ISJC taught about 78 per cent of the pupils in private schools. Thanks to the publication of regular census material by ISIS (1995), and a growing amount of academic research (e.g. Walford, 1993) we now know much more about these schools than we once did. However, with nearly 2500 private schools in the United Kingdom, ISIS/ISJC only account for about half of the total number of private schools. Well over a thousand schools are not included, and very little is known about these schools beyond that they are very varied and tend to be considerably smaller than most other private schools.

One of the groups of private schools not included within the ISIS/ISJC group is the new Christian schools. These schools share an ideology of Biblically-based evangelical Christianity that seeks to relate the message of the Bible to all aspects of present day life whether personal, spiritual or educational. These schools have usually been set up by parents or a church group to deal with a growing dissatisfaction with what is seen as the increased secularism of the great majority of schools. The schools aim to provide a distinctive Christian approach to every part of school life and the curriculum and, usually, parents have a continuing role in the management and organization of the schools.

As there is no national organization overseeing these new Christian schools, it is difficult to trace their emergence, but it would appear that the first school of this type to open in Britain was in Rochester in 1969 (O'Keeffe, 1992). A few more new Christian schools followed in the 1970s, but it was not until the early 1980s that substantial growth occurred. In 1980 there were about ten such schools, but by 1992 there were nearly 90. The growth in popularity of these schools is shown in the increase in the number of pupils in each school as well as the total number of schools. Several schools that opened with just a handful of pupils have rapidly increased to cater for over a hundred. According to Deakin (1989), the main constraint on further expansion for many of these schools is a limitation in the physical space available in the existing premises rather than any lack of potential pupils. This demand for places must be understood in the light of evangelical Christianity being (at that time) one of the fastest growing religious group in Britain.

For several reasons the exact number of schools is difficult to determine. One factor is that the number is continually changing as new schools open and existing ones close, but more important is the lack of any strict definition of what should count as a new Christian school and the absence of any overall organization representing the schools. Some schools are linked to small Christian sects, and have no wish to be associated with any other schools. Others believe their own situation is very different from most of new Christian schools, and do not feel there is any benefit to be gained from associating with them.

About 65 of these schools have, however, come together through mutual recognition into a loose grouping through the Christian Schools Trust (CST). As the number of schools increased during the 1980s, several heads of the schools began to meet together regularly but informally for Christian fellowship and to discuss matters of common interest. More formal meetings and some conferences began to be held, and other teaching staff became involved such that, by 1988, a decision was made to establish a separate Christian Schools Trust 'to promote and assist in the founding of further schools' (CST, 1988). The Trust also provides assistance in the development of curriculum materials, helps coordinate the dissemination of such materials, provides some in-service training for teachers and organized conferences.

Although there is variety within the schools involved with the Christian Schools Trust, the image that the Trust presents tends to be that of charismatic Christianity where considerable emphasis is given to the gifts of the Holy Spirit such as 'speaking in tongues' and 'healing'. New Christian schools without such an emphasis thus tend not to be included. As the results of the survey show, these schools are not part of the mainstream private sector, but are schools with very different educational purposes and philosophy from the bulk of the private sector.

Research methods

This chapter describes various aspects of the nature of the Christian schools with links to the Christian Schools Trust and thus with the Christian Schools Campaign. It is based on an interview and questionnaire survey conduced in 1993. The sampling frame for the research was the September 1992 address list of schools in contact with the Christian Schools Trust. This contained 65 schools, including the junior and senior parts of two schools listed separately and had a degree of independence from one another. With such a small population it was decided to try to obtain information from each school on the list. The results presented here draw on visits to a sample of schools where headteachers were interviewed and postal questionnaires to the remainder of the schools in the group. Eleven schools were visited, selected for reasons of geographical convenience and to give a range of different types of school. All of the schools contacted agreed to a visit and all but one of the interviews with the heads were tape-recorded. The interviews were semi-structured, and information was obtained on the curriculum, discipline, governance and policy matters as well as basic information on the school's pupils and staff. Heads were encouraged to talk at length about the educational philosophy of the school, the reasons why the school was established and the links between the school's philosophy and the curriculum and teaching methods used.

While at the schools some brief observations were made of the school environment, teaching methods and ethos and some other staff were questioned. The extent and nature of these observations varied with the circumstances of each visit, such that a few lessons were observed in some schools while, in others, there was only the chance to be given a tour. Although brief and unsystematic, such observation did allow the gathering of some limited information on the nature and state of the buildings, the size of classrooms, the ethnic and age mix of pupils, and the general atmosphere of the school. Any special features, such as the display of Christian posters, were noted. In general, observation focused on the question, 'what particular characteristics of this school show that it is a Christian school?'

A questionnaire was developed after most of the visits and interviews had been conducted. Questions were drawn up which covered a range of areas similar to those of the interviews, and the structure and wording of the questionnaire was assisted through the comments of two heads previously interviewed. A copy of the questionnaire was sent to all schools on the 1992 Christian Schools Trust address list that had not already been visited.

The dispatch procedure followed that usually recommended. In addition to the questionnaire, the first mailing included a stamped addressed envelope and covering letter. The initial response was low, with only 14 completed questionnaires being returned. The author of one long letter wished to have more information about how the results were to be used before completing the questionnaire. A reminder letter (sent three weeks after the first) gave more information about the project, stressed that interviews and visits had already been conducted at several schools and mentioned two names of people closely involved with the Christian Schools Trust who had already given help. The letter made it clear that the research was independent of the Trust, but that those closely involved with the Trust had been supportive. This resulted in a further 19 completed questionnaires being returned. One head asked for a second copy.

The second reminder (sent a further four weeks later) included a new copy of the questionnaire, a revised covering letter and post-paid return envelope. This posting was shortly before a visit to the Trust's four day Conference held at Easter 1993 in North Wales. Apart from the additional information that attendance at the Conference gave about the schools and the Trust, it was also possible to encourage some of those who had not returned questionnaires to do so. Nine more replies were received following the second reminder.

By combining the interviews and questionnaires, detailed information was received from a total of 53 schools from 65 on the Christian Schools Trust list. However, the returns informed us that two of the schools had closed since the list had been constructed. In one case the questionnaire was still completed and this school's return has been included, while in the other case it was just stated that the school had closed and this school has not been included. The achieved response rate is thus most reasonably calculated as 83 per cent (53 out of 64) which is unusually high. From additional information gathered about the non-responding schools, there is no reason to suspect that those questionnaires returned were unrepresentative of the whole population of schools linked to the Trust. Moreover, it is possible that the achievable response rate was actually higher than this, as some other schools on the list may also have closed. Informal interviews conducted at the Christian Schools Trust Conference in 1993 gave reason to believe that at least two more had closed. The lack of certainty from those centrally involved in the Trust is an indication of the looseness of the group as a whole. These officials would no doubt also have been surprised by the vehemence of a response from one of the schools on the list that stated that they

10

did not wish to be associated in any way with the Trust!

Further background documentary materials on the schools were collected from the Trust itself, and were requested from schools via the questionnaire or interview visits. The various prospectuses and reports on schools were particularly useful as they were aimed at audiences other than researchers - usually prospective parents - and thus presented information in a rather different form. However, while perceptions and presentation may differ according to context, it is to be expected that this particular group of Christian educators would not intentionally lie to researchers. A very high value is put on Christian morality within the schools, so the validity of the responses should be unusually high in terms of the respondents' perceptions of the truth. The responses may still be subject to error, 'economy with the truth', misperceptions and alternative interpretations of events, but intentional falsehood is likely to be low.

The nature of the schools

Although all the schools in the survey held in common high Christian principles and the belief that their schools could provide a more appropriate Christian education than the local state-maintained schools, there was still great diversity between the individual schools in the group. The oldest of the schools opened in 1969, and was for many years the only school of its type. The next oldest started in 1974, and it was another four years before the third. The movement began to gain momentum in 1979 when three schools were started, and during the 1980s there were new schools in the group opening every year. The trend peaked in 1986 when nine opened in the same year. In the 1990s there have been about two new schools opening every year, but there have also been closures. As will be explained later, the fragile financial situations of some of these schools mean that continued existence is not certain - even where the schools are popular and full.

The survey found that the schools ranged considerably in size from less than ten to nearly two hundred children, with a total of more than 3000 children in the 53 schools responding to the survey. Table 2.1 shows the distribution of size of school, and it can be seen that most of the schools had less than 60 pupils, but that there was another substantial group of ten schools that have over 100 children.

Table 2.1

Size of schools

Number of children	<20	21-40	41-60	61-80	81-100	>100
Number of schools	11	11	15	3	3	10
Percentage	21	21	28	6	6	19

All except two of the schools had primary aged children. The two that did not were secondary schools linked with a separate primary school. About half of the schools catered for primary age children only, but the rest usually taught the full compulsory school age range up to 16. Class sizes were usually smaller, and staff/student ratios better than in state-maintained schools. One of the schools explained this in terms of:

> The maximum class size we would ever have is 12, because that was Jesus' maximum class size. (I.4)

Most of the schools were supported by a church, but a significant number were started by ad hoc groups of like-minded parents. Those that were initiated by a church tended to have elders and pastors from that church on their governing body, whereas those started by parents tended to be governed by parents.

As will be explained more fully in the next chapter, the particular precipitating reasons for starting each school were varied, as were the processes by which they became established. Usually, however, there was a mixture of positive reasons based on the belief that parents had responsibility for their children's education and negative reasons concerned with perceived problems with the schools available locally. Typical general reasons for starting the schools given on the questionnaires were:

> One particular set of parents could not find any suitable Christian school for their child in central London, so decided to establish one along with the support of other like-minded parents. (Q.10)

> To give parents a Christian alternative to state education. A system which worked in partnership between home, school and church. (Q.4)

> We were appalled at the lack of quality in state schools and wanted our

children to experience Christian truth in every part of their lives. We wanted to obey God's command to educate our children in Him. We wanted to nurture our children in order that they might be stronger. (Q.22)

From the questionnaires and interviews it is striking that the new Christian schools are the result of a grass-roots movement in education that stems from the belief that education is the responsibility of the parent and the church rather than the state. It is argued that the school should be an extension of the values and beliefs taught within the home and church. For example, in its prospectus, one school stated this as:

The basic responsibility for education lies with parents. The well known proverb 'Train a child the way he should go, and when he is old he will not turn from it' (Proverbs 22:6) is addressed primarily to parents. There are regular parents' meetings to encourage a close relationship between home and school.

The school is seen as an extension of the values and beliefs taught within the home and church. Deakin (1989), who is Head of one of the schools, argues that the human-centred philosophy that dominates the majority of schools in this country is evident throughout the entire curriculum of those schools, and that it shapes the value systems and philosophical frameworks within which all the disciplines are taught. Further:

our schools tend to reflect our society, where there is increasing secularisation, a rising materialism and excessive individualism. Alongside this there is unremitting evidence of a profound lack of respect for authority, and chaos in the area of personal values and morality.

Religious education itself is often of particular concern to the parents involved in these schools. It is argued that the secularization of most schools has led to a commitment to a multi-faith approach to religious education, where religions are examined through their observable characteristics rather than in terms of faith, belief and commitment. This approach is seen to encourage a secular and aridly sceptical view of life and to devalue all faiths other than that of secular humanism.

13

Such a view was common among all of those interviewed. For example, one respondent explained the perceived need for a specifically Christian school in the following way.

> We believe in a Christ-centred curriculum. That there should not be a split, a divide, between the home and family and the school - that their education should be an extension of what they learn at home. We obviously have Christ and the Bible at the centre at home, and we want them to have the same at school.

> I think the divide between Christian education and state education has become far, far greater over recent years - humanism is taught. And not only in the curriculum, but in terms of what children learn in the playground...

As the schools are designed to enable parents to provide a 'biblically-based' Christian education for their children it is to be expected that most of the pupils will be sons or daughters of active Christians. This was, indeed, the case with some 85 per cent of the pupils coming from Christian homes. But most of the schools are also prepared to accept a proportion of pupils from non-Christian families. At the time of the survey, 71 per cent of the schools with secondary age pupils had some children from non-Christian families. Only half of the schools catering only for primary pupils had any children from non-Christian families. This included a very small proportion of pupils from Muslim, Hindu or Sikh families, who valued the religious character of the schools, even if it was not their own. As one school explained,

> Some self professing non-Christian parents can be very supportive of God fearing aims and ethos. (Q.16)

A few of the schools were established with Christian evangelism as an explicit aim, and accept a large proportion of pupils from non-Christian families.

In contrast, about one fifth of the schools did not accept any children from non-Christian homes. Two such schools explained their position thus:

> Our school is not seen as evangelistic, but to provide a 'Kingdom education' for our children. (Q.1)

14

They (non-Christian children) certainly bring with them a set of attitudes/values that are not consistent with the schools. (Q.9)

The flavour and diversity of the schools are best understood through a few example descriptions. The following accounts are not selected to be 'typical', but to show the range and variability. The first example is one of the larger schools within the group that opened in September 1984 with 24 children, and now has expanded to cater for about 130 children aged between five and 16. Its 100 primary age pupils are housed in a redundant 1950s church, situated in a council housing estate. The buildings have been adapted and renovated to provide classrooms, offices, hall, staffroom and so on, and now look very similar to many state maintained primary schools. The facilities are of a reasonable standard, but the school is not lavishly equipped. Its provision is far from the form of elite education often associated with private schools. This school was established by a group of four local Biblically-based evangelical Christian fellowships and serves families of mixed social-class origins. It provides an education that centres around the desire to teach children to grow in a personal relationship with God. Its curriculum is integrated and topic based rather than subject based. Within the overall topic of Justice and Righteousness, for example, the top juniors might study the Stewardship of Creation, including pollution of the environment, destruction of rain forests and similar issues. The focus is on the child knowing God, knowing His created world and knowing other people. The school has six full-time staff, about six others sharing classes on a morning or afternoon basis, and about 20 more part-time staff. Although the school has a few children from non-Christian families, the majority are from families within the local fellowships. The general expectation is that parents with children at the school will donate ten per cent of their income, but this does not allow teachers to be paid full salaries. Payment to teaching staff is thus made according to need.

A second school linked to the Christian Schools Trust provides a clear contrast. It is situated in an area with a large local Asian population, and the majority of the 120 primary-age pupils at the school are from Muslim, Hindu or Sikh families. Only 10 per cent are from Christian homes. Yet all of the teachers are Christian, and the Head's aim is that the school should provide 'a good education and a Christian education'. The school has set fees that allow the staff to be paid on the same salary scale as teachers in the state system. Non-Christian parents choose this school for their children because of its ordered and disciplined environment and because they prefer their children to be in a religiously-based school (even if it is not their own), rather than the secular local state-maintained schools.

The school uses an old church building and is reasonably spacious, with most of the classes in separate rooms. However, two of the classes have to share a large hall separated from one another by temporary room dividers. At playtime the children walk to the local park some ten minutes away. The Christian emphasis is evident in all areas of school life, and is reflected in the wall posters with Bible quotations that decorate the classroom walls. In interview the Head emphasised the importance of the Creation story to his understanding of the Christian message and had spent two years speaking about Genesis Chapter One in the school assemblies.

Funding and staffing

In the main, these schools are not well funded and do not serve traditional high social-class users of the private sector. A few do charge fees that compare with other private preparatory or secondary schools and can provide full salaries to teachers at the nationally agreed levels. But the majority of the schools have low indicative fees or rely on donations from parents that are related to their ability to pay. These schools often live a life of financial uncertainty or, as they would explain it, the schools survive 'on faith'.

The financial situation of many of the schools is precarious. Over the last few years the total number of schools with links to the Christian Schools Trust has remained relatively constant, but this is due to new schools replacing an annual loss of two or three schools. Most of the schools would not be able to operate if it were not for many teachers who give their time free.

Seventy-four per cent of the schools have the status of a charity, and 57 per cent rely partly on a church to fund them. Most of the schools do not receive support from any other trusts or charities apart from the church, but some do.

A small minority of the schools rely almost totally on freewill gifts to finance the school, but most have some sort of fee structure. However, only 21 per cent set fees the same for all children, the majority have a system that takes into account how much parents can afford. Some examples of answers to a question on the fee structure were,

Church members pay less than those from other churches or from non-church affiliation. (Q.11)

The church pays for the staff, and the parents pay for the curriculum, heating and lighting. (Q.29)

Ideally the fees would cover the costs of running the school, but so many parents have found themselves in financial difficulties lately that this is no longer so; therefore we rely on gifts to survive month by month. (Q.35)

The parent contributions meet the majority of the running costs. This leaves the difference to be prayed in. (Q.38)

There is a set fee structure with reductions for second or subsequent children of the same family. However, personal financial difficulties are discussed with our financial advisor. (Q.33)

The survey showed that there were more than 610 teachers working in the new Christian schools. Changing circumstances and gaps in the data mean that figures are indicative rather than exact. Most of the schools have a mixture of part-time and full-time teachers with those working part-time often being parents and receiving no pay at all. Of the roughly 610 teachers, just under half were in this part-time unpaid category. Even among the full-time staff there were some who were not paid. Of the 200 or so full time staff, some 80 per cent were paid something while about 20 per cent were not paid at all. Teachers were unpaid sometimes because they did not require any additional family income or sometimes because they 'lived by faith' and relied on voluntary gifts from parents, the church or others. There were also approximately 130 part-time teachers who receive some pay. However, even where teachers were paid, the majority were on salaries lower than that they would have obtained in the state sector.

As Christian faith is central to the mission of these schools it is to be expected that all the teachers would be Christians. This is one area where the new Christian schools are uniform - they will not hire a non-Christian to teach. As the schools are private, the teachers do not have to have qualified teacher status to teach, and there is considerable variety between the schools in the nature of the qualifications held by teachers. However, the majority of full-time teachers had qualified teacher status, and there was a fair sprinkling of higher degrees. Many had extensive experience of state-maintained schools before becoming involved in these new Christian schools, sometimes at the level of Head or Deputy Head. In contrast, many of the part-time teachers are not qualified in an academic sense, but here the Christian schools tend to see belief as more important than qualifications. In fact, for some of the schools, if a person had been 'called by God' to teach, that was the only qualification needed.

Curriculum

Private schools do not have to teach the National Curriculum, and most of these Christian schools did not follow the National Curriculum framework. Eleven per cent of those schools responding to the survey said they taught the National Curriculum in full, 30 per cent said they taught most of it, 23 per cent said they did not teach much of it and 36 per cent said simply that they did not teach the National Curriculum. There was little difference in attitude to the National Curriculum between those schools started and governed by a church and those started and governed by parents. In the first case 41 per cent of the church-based schools taught all or most of the National Curriculum, compared to 36 per cent of the parent-based schools. Several schools saw following the National Curriculum as posing problems for the new Christian schools:

> The SATs would bring too much dominance of the objective led curriculum and not allow room for staff to explore and develop the unique features of a Christian curriculum in the early stages of establishing the school. (Q.16)

> Expense, especially of moderation. Last year we were informed they cost £300 a day and came in pairs! (Q.6)

As well as the practical difficulties of meeting the demands of the National Curriculum, there are certain ideological problems for the schools:

> Christian curriculum is the whole curriculum (i.e. not just a matter of evolution, sex and R.E!!). We challenge the 'myth of neutrality', the supposed value neutrality of the secular curriculum in state schools. (Q.18)

18

Parents at our school have developed their own biblically based curriculum. In many areas this is not in conflict with the National Curriculum regarding, in particular, the knowledge aspects. But the approach, the interpretation and the secular framework pose difficulties for full implementation. (Q.40)

The degree to which the schools are willing to teach the National Curriculum is linked to their beliefs about the need for a 'God-centred' curriculum, and their depth of thinking about the nature of knowledge. Sometimes the curriculum is virtually the same as that in state schools, and children study for the same GCSE subjects, but in others the whole nature of the curriculum has been rethought such that God and Christ are given priority. Thirty-six per cent of the schools made use of Accelerated Christian Education (ACE) learning materials (discussed in the next section), while others were developing a wider range of teaching/learning materials that project a Christ-centred curriculum. Other Christian curriculum materials such as 'Lifepack' are also used.

Sixty-four per cent of the schools do not use ACE materials at all. Some use other types of specifically Christian teaching materials, but they tend to have a more traditional classroom approach to teaching. In these cases standard commercial textbooks and teaching materials are usually used, but often in a judicious way which may involve vetting. Books are selected and rejected according to the belief system they reflect as well as the academic subject matter. One head of a primary school explained:

We have various different curriculums we use. A lot of them we have vetted, a lot of them we have taken bits out. Cut bits out. We use the Ginn reading scheme...and a lot of it we had to take out. A lot of it we were very unhappy with. We've taken out any bits to do with witches, a lot of Ginn has got the supernatural underlined to it - a lot of myths. I can't remember, we took out a lot about spirits that live in bogs and a lot of ghosts and haunting all that sort of thing in it. We were very unhappy with that, but it is the best overall.

Interviewer: How do the children react to that? Most children would want to know - 'what have they cut out?'

Answer: No they don't! They don't worry about what has been cut out. I think because we've got such a good relationship with our parents and the standards that are set at home church and school are so clear, that these

19

children would not particularly want to read about those things. Every book is read by a parent or teacher before it is allowed into the school. To make sure that they are suitable book to have in the school. Occasionally we miss things, and we've had children come up and say - I don't like this story, do you think it should still be in the school? And we have actually taken out some at the children's request - and they are not 'religious' children - they are very normal children. (I.3)

But, while Christian teaching is given prominence, many of the schools also have a strong emphasis on academic success. The schools are often attractive to both Christian and non-Christian families because they offer a highly ordered and disciplined environment and have teachers who are dedicated to the best interests of the children in their care. This emphasis on obedience and discipline is reflected in the retention by most of the schools of the right to use corporal punishment. It is not used lightly, and on interview heads often could only cite a few instances where a cane or similar had been used, but it was seen as a necessary last resort. Nearly all the schools also had schools uniform, although in some cases it was extremely simple.

There are some other features of the curriculum that distinguish these schools. All but one school taught Biblical creation as fact. Two-thirds of the schools taught evolution as well as creation, but all of them treated it as a theory. In nearly all cases it was taken for granted that the Bible's account of six day creation was literally true, and the evolutionary view was false.

We present the facts to the children, and it's obvious what's right and what's wrong. (I.2)

[Evolution is taught] Only as a discredited theory..... children have to know why so many books, programmes, etc. say such things as dinosaurs lived millions of years before man 'evolved'. (Q.22)

One head explained,

Interviewer: Are you totally literal about it, six days and so on?
Yes, my only question would be, why did God take so long. Yes, of course there are some Christians who go for a gap theory, but we believe it was six days. (I.8)

20

Not all the schools taught in a way that takes creation for granted, some are more open to debate between the conflicting opinions and look at evolution and creation together:

> If the children ask about it we compare the basic ideas of evolution with creation, pointing out the questions people have on both sides. (Q.3)

Sex education is another area of difference between many of these schools and state-maintained schools. Sex education was not taught in 42 per cent of the schools. Fifty-seven per cent of the schools did teach the subject, and the usual approach was by starting with the family:

> The facts of the subject are taught in Biology classes. Ethical issues which relate to this topic are dealt with in Religious Studies and English lessons. (Q.23)

> In the context of biblical principles of marriage. (Q.24)

Those schools that did not teach sex education saw this area as not being within the sphere of the school's responsibility:

> We'd rather the parents did it. (I.1)

> We only teach it as it arises. Policy is that it's the parents' job, but we will answer a straight question with a straight answer, in practice this does happen. (Q.6)

Accelerated Christian Education

A rather different sub-group of schools within the Christian Schools Trust group has a controversial history, and suffered badly in the press following poor reports from HM Inspectors during 1985 when at least four new Christian schools were served with notices of complaint (e.g. DES, 1985). Areas of concern within these reports included inadequate and unsafe accommodation, lack of resources, unstimulating environments, and inadequate curriculum. In all these four reports, however, the Accelerated Christian Education (ACE) teaching programme used by the schools was a common area of concern.

The survey showed that thirty-six per cent (19 schools) used Accelerated Christian Education (ACE) materials to a varying extent, and a few use little else. As explained in detail elsewhere (Walford, 1991), ACE is a highly standardized system of individualized instruction developed in the United States, where all the information, materials and equipment necessary to set up and run a Christian school are provided. Pupils work at their own paces through a series of Packs of Accelerated Christian Education (PACEs) which are provided for each different subject area. They sit in separate cubicles which are designed to limit student interaction by having vertical screens between pupils. Students can gain the attention of their supervisor or monitor by raising one of two or three small flags provided for each pupil. When an exercise is finished, the pupils mark their own work at a testing station. According to Rose (1988), by about 1987 ACE was used in 5000 schools in the United States and a further 600 schools in 86 other countries. Rose (1988: 117) describes ACE as 'having taken the scientific management of schools to the extreme. Their model more closely approximates to that of the factory or office: there are "supervisors" and "monitors" rather than "teachers"; student "offices" rather than desks; and "testing stations" that create "quality control".'

Her Majesty's Inspectors described the ACE scheme in the following way:

In each subject the programme consists of some 140 to 150 numbered workbooks (PACEs), and the pupils proceed from one to the next in order. Pupils are said to complete on average a total of 20 pages per day, but this will vary considerably from pupil to pupil. 23. In general PACEs consist of a series of information passages each followed by exercises based on it. In mathematics these exercises consist of formal computations, sometimes expressed as 'problems'; in other subjects they take the form of questions requiring brief answers, lists to be matched or sentences in which missing words have to be supplied or certain words have to be underlined or similarly annotated...

24. Each workbook contains one or more intermediate 'check-up tests' and a concluding 'PACE test'. The exercises and check up tests are completed in pencil and scored by the pupils themselves from answer books kept at the central 'scoring station'. Errors are

erased and new answers written in until all are correct... (DES, 1985)

Largely similar descriptions of the ACE learning environment, process and curriculum are given in all four DES reports of the ACE schools inspected during January and February 1985, and are echoed by Skinner (1981) in his description of Emmanuel Christian School, Fleetwood, which he visited in 1981. More strikingly, a very similar description is given by Rose (1988) in her study of an American ACE school that she calls 'The Academy'.

ACE seems to have had two pathways into Britain. The first was through a group of Americans linked to the Brentwaters American Air Force Base in Suffolk who first formed Faith Christian Church and in September 1980 opened Faith Christian Academy (DES, 1985a), which, at the time of inspection the school, made almost exclusive use of ACE and served only American children. ACE's second pathway into Britain was through Fleetwood Full Gospel Church, which opened Emmanuel Christian School in 1979. The church had been considering establishing a day school for some years, and the discovery of ACE materials and methods allowed them to proceed. By 1981 there were about 70 pupils (Skinner, 1981). The Principal of the school, Dr Michael Smith, who was also British coordinator of ACE, viewed Emmanuel as a 'pilot school' and, through conferences and visits, actively encouraged other reformed Church groups to establish their own schools using ACE. He met with considerable success, with six churches taking his advice by early 1981.

ACE teaching materials and methods were an important part of the growth of some of these new Christian schools, for the existence of ACE enabled small groups of Christian parents to contemplate providing all age Christian schooling for their children at low cost and with little or no teaching experience required by those adults in charge. In particular, ACE allows schools to teach the entire age range of children without the need for specialist teachers in each subject area at the secondary level. The survey showed that 46 per cent of the schools with secondary age children made use of some ACE materials, while only 17 per cent of the primary only schools did so. Only 16 per cent of ACE using schools restricted their age range to primary. Clearly, extending the age range to secondary presented fewer problems for ACE schools than others, for ACE enabled them to provide what they took to be a full subject curriculum even where the number of children involved was low.

Table 2.2 shows that church based schools were more likely to use ACE than those started by parents.

Table 2.2
Schools using ACE materials (percentages)

	Church based	Parent based	Both or other	Total
ACE-using	41	9	47	36
Non-ACE-using	59	91	53	64

Table 2.3 shows that ACE-using schools were less likely to take children from non-Christian backgrounds, and less likely to teach sex education at the school.

Table 2.3
Differences between ACE and non-ACE schools (percentages)

	ACE-using	Non-ACE-using
Have non-Christians	58	68
Only Christians	42	32
Teach sex education	42	67
No sex education	58	33

In practice, the heavy criticism of the method from HMIs and others has meant that many of the newer schools in the group have never used ACE. Schools are now involved in developing their own materials and, even where used, in most schools ACE methods no longer dominate the learning process. However, some of the schools associated with the Trust still see ACE as central to their vision of Christian education (Dennett, 1988), and believe that its emphasis on ordered independent learning rather than whole-class teaching reflects and reinforces Christian discipline and the Christian message. The use of ACE materials thus was a potential cause of tension within the group of new Christian schools. Some Heads were firmly against the whole concept of individualized learning especially through this particular system. Others believed that it was inappropriate for their own school, but were not opposed in principle. One head explained,

We know about the ACE and we think they are super people. We didn't start that way, and we don't believe it's right for here. (I.1)

In contrast, some schools associated with the Trust see ACE's emphasis on ordered independent learning rather than whole-class teaching as reflecting and reinforcing Christian discipline and the Christian message.

We are committed to ACE...we use it as fully as we can. (Q. 28)

Other schools still see many merits in the philosophy behind the ACE system, but have gradually adapted their use of it:

We decided that we would use an individualized learning system - a system called Accelerated Christian Education. And it would be a tool that we would use, although we did not become what is called 'an ACE school'. But we used it as a tool as well as class teaching - group teaching. And, over the years, we have been developing our own curriculum, and gradually moving off ACE.

It had many principles that attracted us. I think the fact that pupils would learn at their own rate and that there was a personal responsibility and a personal discipline involved in setting daily workloads and so forth. Making students more responsible for their work and it being a goal that they had to achieve and, if not, it was homework, tended to be a good incentive.

It was used as one of the tools really. It did influence our approach, because it put the focus on learning rather than teaching continually, and we were all experienced teachers and it caused the teacher to see and act in a different role - more of a servant - rather than just the one who has all knowledge and spout forth - which can be rather ego-building. You know, there is that role of the teacher to impart knowledge, but equally there is that role to serve the pupils. (I.9)

One of the problems with ACE materials is that they are American based and reflect that society rather than British society. This particular school still uses ACE materials within some subject teaching, but has reacted to this and other problems by working to produce British-based ACE-type learning materials. They retain much of the ACE individualized philosophy.

Conclusion

The survey showed that the new Christian schools are a diverse group. Even when looking at those that have come together under the Christian Schools Trust, there are many differences evident within the group.

The first main area where the schools differ is to whom they open their doors. In practically all of the schools the majority of the children are from Christian homes, but most of the schools allow a limited number of children from non-Christian families to attend the school. Those that do not do so, see the schools as operating for the benefit of the children of the Church only and not the children of the world. In contrast, are the schools that believe that the schools should be open to all children, and see an intake of non-Christian children as a positive evangelistic opportunity - a chance to convert unbelievers to Christianity.

The second main point of difference within the new Christian schools is concerned with their governorship. Some of the schools believe that for the school to be truly Christian it must be governed by a Church, and seen as a branch of the ministry of that Church. In these cases the ministers and elders of the Church are usually the governors of the school and the Church is likely to give substantial financial and other support. Other schools focus on the belief that the responsibility for the education of children lies with parents, and the governing body is dominated by parents. These schools would not want the Church leadership to have authority over parents in the running of the school.

The third main area where schools differ is their choice of curriculum. At one extreme are the schools that do not use anything other than ACE materials, and who reject the National Curriculum as secular and humanistic. On the other extreme are some schools that teach practically all of the National Curriculum, and believe that it is possible to do so from a Christian perspective. These last schools that closely follow the National Curriculum tend to see ACE as alien and alienating for children.

During interview, one of the Headteachers expressed this diversity in the following terms:

I am very aware that there are *such* differences between the Christian schools up and down the land. To keep them together in any shape or form through the Trust... is quite a remarkable feat. And also to claim Divine Inspiration for all these varieties is also quite a feat! But God is a God of diversity.(I.7)

Yet the schools are not simply a collection of independent schools with no unifying factors. There are several interlinked common factors that provide a basis for unity, and all of these indicate a basic philosophy and world view that is radically different from that found in most other schools. Although they would not necessarily see any division, the schools have both Christian and academic aims. Most schools claim to be concerned with questions of behaviour and morality as well as academic success, but these schools have the propagation of Christian thinking at the centre of their objectives. All of the teachers in the new Christian schools are themselves Christian and believe that the Bible and the message of Christianity are relevant for today. The schools attempt to teach children to live according to Biblical principles, and the teachers provide role models for belief and behaviour. They seek to pass on the children not only knowledge about the Bible, but belief in its truth and belief in Jesus Christ.

These factors enable the schools to achieve their common aim 'to train a child the way he should go, and when he is old he will not turn from it.' The teachers believe that the way children should be trained is the Christian way, and that this will only happen in schools where Christianity is central to all that the schools do. They believe that only in Biblically-based schools will the Biblical instruction be followed. The diversity between the schools is thus less substantial than might first be thought, for the variability can be interpreted as simply differing interpretations of how to implement schooling that has Christianity at its centre. If God is a 'God of diversity', then it is to be expected that Christian schools will vary.

3 Why start a school?

Introduction

Interviews with headteachers and others involved in establishing new schools showed that there was considerable variety in the precipitating reasons and in the processes by which they had been established. One well-informed headteacher explained this in the following way:

> At one time a lot of Christian schools started because there was a lot happening in other schools that Christians weren't happy with. So there were the obvious things such as halloween, some of the areas of sex education, obvious areas of RE, obvious areas of worship, evolution, creation. And parents would say this is causing concern. I mean I could give you a list of things that have happened even recently, and locally. We've had children in schools where they've had a whole day given over to fortune telling. We've had children putting needles into dolls... There are schools where they've been making prayer mats and praying to monkey gods. Now these are clear things that as Christians we get concerned about and object about. We also object that evolution is taught as a fact and not as a theory...

> The Bible says that we should train up our children in the way they should go... I don't have to have a special reason to put my children, as a father, in a Christian school. For I am simply doing what God want me to do - to train the children up - my children - in the way that they should go.

Everything is based on God's will. Now how could I obey that command to train up my children the way they should go when so much of their five day a week schooling is against those standards or, at the very least, is not based on them? So for that positive reason I need to put my children in a place where the standards and attitudes and the ethos are in sympathy with what I would teach at home. It is the family, church and school that work together for the child... (I.7)

This chapter will examine in more detail this range of reasons for starting new Christian private schools. Understanding the perspectives of those involved is a necessary precursor to a fuller discussion of the Christian schools movement and the resulting pressure group.

The Biblical justification

This section will attempt to present an outline of the theological basis for the new Christian schools put forward as a justification by the schools themselves. This task is not an easy one. It has already been shown that there is considerable diversity in the nature of the schools that have links with the Christian Schools Trust, and there is a corresponding diversity in their theological understandings. Further, even within each school, it is unlikely that there will be complete agreement among all staff and parents (and church officials where they are closely involved) about theological issues. Disputes over theological interpretation as it impinges on the running of schools are not uncommon. During the period of the research, there were several examples of schools loosing significant teachers and breaking links to churches as a result of differing theological interpretations.

However, all of the schools claim that they are 'Biblically based' schools, and many of those closely involved in the schools interpret sections of the Bible as a distinct justification for separate Christian schools. Their attitudes towards the Bible and the general nature of their belief also sets them apart from the mainstream of much of present day Christian belief. Thus, while there is diversity within the group, most outsiders would probably view this diversity as small compared with the similarities. The very fact that the parents involved with these Christian schools reject the schooling that is provided by the state on religious grounds, sets them apart from most Christians.

The sources to be used in this discussion of the theological justifications for the new Christian schools are several, but only a small indicative sample will be examined here. They all emphasise the 'official' view rather than the 'theology in action' that might be presented by parents or teachers in the schools. Being a grassroots movement, the new Christian schools have not usually come into being as the direct result of deep theological reflection; those involved are not highly trained theologians. It would appear that, in general, the development of a rigorous theological justification for the schools and for Christian education has occurred as much after establishment of the schools as before. The everyday pressures of running a school mean that some of those involved did not see the development of a deep theological justification as a first priority.

One source of information on the theological basis for the schools was the survey of the new Christian schools discussed in chapter 2. As these questionnaires and interviews were completed by or conducted with the heads of the schools, the view is clearly the 'official' one that the head wished to put forward for public consumption. Another source of information is the materials produced by these schools in the form of prospectuses and other documentation, and the Christian Schools Trust newsletter which appears three times each year. Books which discuss and argue for the establishment of Christian schools are another very important source. Christian schools thrive in USA, Canada and Australia, and there is thus a plethora of published materials in English which argue the case for Christian schools. There are also a some books which originate in Great Britain, and a very few books written by people directly associated with these new Christian schools. For the sake of brevity, this section will consider one book written by an ex-Headteacher of one of the schools central to the Trust, one book written by a widely respected 'guru' on Christian education and some of the materials published by the schools themselves.

But first there is the problem of the general description of the beliefs held by those involved. One word often applied by others to the sort of Christian belief exemplified by those involved with these schools is 'fundamentalist'. This is not the word usually applied by those people involved for, particularly since the Salman Rushdie affair, it has become a label which has collected around it some very negative associations of extremism. However, the Concise Oxford Dictionary's definition of fundamentalism as 'strict maintenance of traditional, orthodox, religious beliefs, such as the inerrancy of Scripture and literal acceptance of the creeds as fundamentals of Protestant Christianity' is one that describes well the theology of many of those associated with these schools.

However, there are other aspects of the concept of fundamentalism which could only be applied to some of the more extreme schools associated with the Trust. Sahgal and Yuval-Davis (1992) argue that there are two features that are common to all fundamentalist religious movements: one, is the claim that their version of religion is the only true one and, two, that they use political means to impose their version of the truth on others. Practically all of these schools accept the first point and would claim that their understanding of Christianity is the only true one. This means that they are usually firmly against any pluralist understandings of religious belief. Indeed, the celebration of festivals related to other religions was one of the strongest reasons why some of these parents had removed their children from state schools. Within the new Christian schools the Gospel is presented as the only valid form of religious belief, and other religions are believed to be simply erroneous. Within this acceptance of the uniqueness of the Christian message there are some who rely very strongly on religious texts and these only, and others who are more experientially based and perhaps linked to charismatic leadership. Within the latter are 'born-again Christians' who prioritise the experiential and who often have only a limited knowledge or understanding of Biblical texts. Some of this range is to be found in the new Christian schools.

However, the second feature of fundamentalism identified by Sahgal and Yuval-Davis (1992) is less often visible. Those involved with the new Christian schools do not use political means to impose their version of the truth on others. In spite of the Christian Schools Campaign springing from the Christian Schools Trust, most of those involved are not particularly 'political' people at all. Although there are a few who are savagely intolerant of other people's views and behaviour and who take an authoritarian stance to teaching and to the role of the state, very few are actively involved in trying to impose their view through political means. The establishment of separate Christian schools is best interpreted as a partial withdrawal from the world. Rather than seeking to change things, the pragmatic response of those involved with the Christian schools is to withdraw.

While the term 'fundamentalist' has its difficulties, the alternative of 'evangelical' which is favoured by many of those involved is also problematic. To be evangelical to many implies that active evangelism is a prominent part of religious activity and belief. A few of the schools were, indeed, established with this aim in mind. Here, schools are designed to bring people into a situation where they hear the Christian message and are given the opportunity to accept it. Thus non-Christian children are taught the Christian message in the hope that they will be converted, and an opportunity is made for the parents and the rest of the family also to be evangelised.

Most of the new Christian schools do not take this attitude. Most of the schools were established by parents or churches to deal with the schooling of children from Christian families. Some of the schools are very firm that they will not accept children from non-Christian families, and some are very scathing about the morality of 'using' children in this way to evangelize non-Christian families. In short, neither 'fundamentalist' or 'evangelical' is an entirely suitable overall description for the theological position of these schools. Most of those involved simply call themselves 'Christian', often with the assumption that it is obvious that this puts them into a different category to that of most voluntary schools or private schools with a religious basis. Those more reticent to condemn others usually use the term 'new Christian' school.

The public and explicit theology of the new Christian schools can be investigated through printed documents. The first document to be considered is a well known book by Harro Van Brummelen (1988) *Walking with God in the Classroom* which has been reprinted several times. Van Brummelen is Associate Professor of Education and Chairperson, Education Division at the private Trinity Western University, British Columbia, Canada. This book is worth examining in detail not only because it was recommended by several of those involved with the schools, but because Van Brummelen was the main invited speaker at the Christian Schools Trust's Christian Education Conference held at Kinmel Hall in April, 1993. This Conference was the key event in the Christian Schools Trust calendar, the previous similar conference being held at University of Nottingham in 1991. During the four day conference, which was attended by over 200 people, Van Brummelen gave five keynote speeches, and it must therefore be assumed that his theology and view of Christian schools is likely to receive strong support within the schools.

In *Walking with God in the Classroom*, Van Brummelen starts out by stating what he believes to be the function of schooling:

I believe that, as much as possible, the function of schooling should be to educate young adults for a life of responsible discipleship in Jesus Christ (p.2).

He then devotes the first chapter to a discussion of what this might mean, focusing on what he sees as the three main agencies of Christian nurture.

The most important agency of Christian nurture is the *family*, the basic building block of society. God directs His injunction to nurture children in the first place to parents (Dt 6:6-9; 11:18-21). Paul adds that parents must bring up children "in the training and instruction of the Lord" (Eph 6:4)...

The second agency of Christian nurture is the *church*. The teaching ministry of the church is emphasized in the book of Acts. Both Peter and Paul taught how God works through history and has fulfilled history with the Good News of Jesus Christ. In Corinth and Ephesus Paul stayed for lengthy periods, teaching the people the Word of God (Acts 18:11; 19:10; 20:13)...

The injunction to nurture children in the Lord goes beyond the family and the church, however. Both Deuteronomy 6 and Psalm 78 also address the people of Israel collectively. Telling "the next generation the praiseworthy deeds of the Lord, His power and the wonders he has done" (Psalm 78:4) is a responsibility shared by the whole Christian community. In Biblical times, "schooling" took place within the extended family and, to a limited extent, in the synagogue. Today, society has become so complex that few homes and no regular church education program can provide adequate general education. Besides, society provides few meaningful full-time roles for adolescents and young adults outside formal education. Schools and colleges therefore have become necessary and influential.

I am personally convinced that Deuteronomy 6 and Psalm 78 imply that in today's pluralistic society distinctly Christian schools are desirable. The Christian ethic that at one time undergirded North American society has all but disappeared. Children must develop thoroughly "Christian minds". That is difficult for the family and for the church to accomplish by themselves with so many counteracting influences in society. We shortchange children's nurture in the Lord if their schooling does not openly proclaim that "the heavens declare the glory of God", and that "the precepts of the Lord are right, giving joy to the heart" (Ps 19:1,8)... (Van Brummelen, 1988: 3-4).

Van Brummelen summarizes his understanding of the roles of the family, church and school as each being one leg of an educational tripod. He argues that

33

children will have difficulty staying in balance if any of the three legs stand on a different base. All three should stand firm on the base of 'the Word of God and the flame of Christ's Spirit'.

Van Brummelen argues that education cannot be neutral, for education is centrally concerned with leading forth and the shaping of attitudes and dispositions. All education is thus to be seen as religious in the sense that it can only be done according to faith commitments and ideals. For Christians, the basic aim must be that of helping children to become 'Kingdom citizens', which means (1), whilst the school has a broader educational task than the church, it must 'proclaim the necessity of heading God's call to repentance, conversion and obedience'; (2) as Kingdom citizens are members of the Body of Christ, Christian schools must be training grounds for communal action; (3) as Kingdom citizens have a mandate to 'make disciples of all nations' Christian schools should encourage students in this calling, not just for the future, but for their time at school as well; (4) as Kingdom citizens live the fruits of love, service and truth, schools should provide constant opportunities for students to put their faith into practice, and (5) Christian schools should, in themselves, be a sign in the secular community.

Although these aims and objectives for schooling do not even mention traditional curriculum areas, the actual curriculum discussed in Van Brummelen's book is far from narrow. He is not concerned to lay out the details of curriculum, but his examples cover all of the main subject as well as some other important areas. Thus ethics, politics, economics, social relations and health, for example, are seen to have a place alongside mathematics, science, and the other traditional subject areas. However, while theses subjects may be taught separately, they also are seen as overlapping, and inter-related. All are seen in the context of what can be discovered about God and what He wishes us to do.

The second source to be investigated as a source of theological justification is a book by Stephen Dennett (1988) *A Case for Christian Education*. After ten years in Church of England primary schools, in 1982, Dennett became Head of the private new Christian King's School, Harpenden. He held that position for six years and was very active in encouraging the formation of new schools, particularly through the use of ACE materials. He now runs the Christian Curriculum Project which aims to 'provide a source of good quality, Biblically-based curriculum, which will help each child to develop his or her own God-given abilities' (CST, 1991: 9). In practice, these materials are developments of ACE materials designed for a British market, and largely follow the workbook structured approach of ACE. The materials are being trialed and used in several of the ACE schools linked to the Christian Schools Trust.

Dennett is neither an academic nor a theologian. His book is written with a very practical emphasis, but there are some important overlaps between his justification for Christian schools and those of Van Brummelen. Some short extracts are sufficient to give the feel of Dennett's writing. He starts the book with a brief account of his own changing experience in state schools, and recounts the way that

> God began to open my eyes to what was written about education in the Bible. As a father, I found that Ephesians 6:4 hit me between the eyes: 'Fathers, do not exasperate your children; instead bring them up in the training and instruction of the Lord.'...The more I read the Bible, the more I realised that *parents*, not the state, were responsible for educating their children. The church, too, had a central role in providing godly teachers and biblically-based curriculum, not only for children in the fellowship, but for the world at large (p. 10).

Dennett argues that the Bible is full of instructions to fathers, older women, parents and church leaders to pass on to the next generation the whole counsel of God (e.g. Ep 6:4; Psm 78:1-8; Tit 2:1-5), and that this cannot be done simply in Sunday schools or church meetings. He states that between 6 and 18 only about 400 hours will have usually be spent in such activities, compared with

> 11,000 hours in secular schools under humanist teachers and 15,000 hours watching television. That is a combination of 26,000 hours of mental programming! In essence, most young people pass into adulthood with a mind mounded by the 'weak and miserable' principles of the world (Gal 4:9) rather than the truth that leads to eternal life. (p. 18)

In a similar way to Van Brummelen, Dennett sees Deuteronomy 6 as one of the most important commandments in the Bible. He quotes Deuteronomy 6: 4-9 in full, and then discusses what he sees as the implications of the passage.

> These commandments that I give you today are to be upon your hearts. Impress them on your children. Talk about them when you sit at home and when you walk along the road, when you lie down and when you get up.

Tie them as symbols on your hands and bind them on your foreheads.

Dennett emphasises that parents are to impress (or 'teach them diligently') the commandments of God on their children, and that the Word of God should be taught all day, every day. If the Bible is the most important book in the world, argues Dennett, then we should write it in the hearts and minds of the next generation.

The third and final sources to be discussed here are some of the materials published by the schools themselves - usually in the form of prospectuses. These tend, probably for reasons of space, to be very simple outlines of the school's justification of the need for separate Christian schools. One typical example from a short prospectus simply states:

> We have a Biblical base for what we are doing:
> Proverbs 1 v 7 'The fear of the Lord is the beginning of wisdom'
> Proverbs 14 v 34 'Righteousness exalts a nation'
> Proverbs 22 v 6 'Train a child in the way he should go and when he is old he will not turn from it'
> Deuteronomy 6 v 5 'Love the Lord your God with all your heart and with all your mind and with all your strength'
> 2 Timothy 3 v 15 'You know that from infancy you have known the Holy Scriptures which are able to make you wise for salvation through faith in Christ Jesus'
> Philippians 4 v 8 'Whatever is true, whatever is noble, whatever is right, whatever is pure, whatever is lovely, what ever is admirable if anything is excellent, or praiseworthy, think about such things.'

Another prospectus states:

> The aim of the school is to provide an education which is firmly based upon Christian principles. This has certain consequences and amongst them are the following:
> # Each child is unique and precious because he or she is created in God's image and must therefore be treated with great care and respect. Class sizes are kept small in order to ensure sufficient time for each child.
> # The model for personal development is that of Jesus Christ, who grew in wisdom (moral, creative and intellectual) and stature (physical) and in

favour with God (spiritual) and man (social) (Luke 2:25)... The child is encouraged to relate correctly to God, to him- or herself, to other people and to the world at large.

The basic responsibility for education lies with parents. The well known proverb 'Train a child the way he should go, and when he is old he will not turn from it' (Proverbs 22:6) is addressed primarily to parents. There are regular parent meetings to encourage a close relationship between home and school.

Even within these examples the diversity of ways in which the Bible is used is apparent. While Dennett, for example, has a very literal, yet selective, view of the instructions given by God to his followers, Van Brummelen takes much greater account of the context in which instructions were given. However, there are several aspects to these justifications that are immediately apparent. The most important point is that these authors suggest that the purpose of education is primarily about passing on the Christian message. This is fundamentally different from the way most parents, teachers and educationists would view the purpose of education and it would appear to mark a deep rift between the ideas behind these documents and mainstream schooling. In practice, however, the distinction is not clear-cut, and in practice all of these documents demonstrate that the new Christian schools actually offer a far wider curriculum that these general statements would imply. Both the legal requirement that parents should 'cause their children to be educated' and the parents' own desires ensure that the curriculum covered is very similar to that in state schools.

A second key aspect of these justifications is that all of the authors argue their view using Biblical quotations. There are differences in the way the Bible is used to support statements and ideas, but it is accepted as authoritative, and the reader is not expected to challenge its inherent authority. While there may be some difficulties in understanding some passages or in applying them to present-day situations, in the minds of these authors, there is no question of the appropriateness of using Biblical quotations to justify arguments. Readers are not expected to question whether writings at least approximately 2000 years old *can* have relevance to modern situations, they are expected to look for and find such relevance. Indeed, all of these authors would probably claim that their prayerful reading of the Bible has led, not to helping them to formulate their own views but, to enabling them to understand more of God's will about education and schooling.

A third aspect worth noting is that the authors use only a limited range of

Biblical quotations to support their views on education and the same texts are used by several of the authors. Most readers of the Bible would agree that there are few Biblical texts that refer specifically to teaching or schooling, yet some of these authors interpret particular texts to have direct relevance not only to education in general, but also to the specific issue of separate Christian schools.

While neither Dennett nor Van Brummelen claim to be completely authoritative interpreters of the Bible, Van Brummelen is 'personally convinced' that there should be separate Christian schools, and Dennett says that it is his 'conviction' that 'new wine needs new wineskins'. But both quote extensively from the Bible and build their argument by selecting quotations from the Bible and then offering their interpretation as the 'obvious' one. Both not only try to justify Christian education as such through Biblical quotation, but also believe that their vision of Christian education required separate Christian schools. In their initial justification for separate schools, both draw upon (amongst other references) Deuteronomy 6, Psalm 78 and Ephesians 6:4. It is worth looking at these three sources in turn.

Deuteronomy 6 follows the story of God giving the Commandments to the people of Israel. God supposedly spoke the words 'in a great voice...out of the fire, the cloud and the thick mist' and gave them to Moses on two tablets of stone. Moses then receives the commandments, statutes and laws which the Lord commanded Moses 'to teach you to observe in the land into which you are passing to occupy it, a land flowing with milk and honey'. It is these commandments that Israel is told to keep in their heart, repeat to their sons and speak of indoors and outdoors, when they lie down and when they rise. They are also told to bind them as a sign on the hand and wear them as a phylactery on the forehead; write them up on the doorposts of their homes and on their gates.

Psalm 78 (especially 1-8) is also used by both Dennett and Van Brummelen to support their case for Christian schools. This psalm starts with an introductory section which reiterates the need for Israel to teach its sons the law. 'From their sons we will not hide the praises of the Lord and his might nor the wonderful acts he has performed; then they shall repeat them to the next generation. He laid on Jacob a solemn charge and established a law in Israel, which he commanded our fathers to teach their sons, that it might be known to a future generation, to children yet unborn, and these would repeat it to their sons in turn' (v.4-6).

Ephesians 6.4 is also used by both Van Brummelen and Dennett to support separate Christian schools. In both cases it is the specific verse that is quoted -

'You fathers, again, must not goad your children to resentment, but give them instruction, and the correction, which belong to a Christian upbringing'. Dennett describes his own book as 'a call to Christian leaders to get involved in the next generation by opening Christian schools. It is a call to Christian parents to fulfill the command of Ephesians 6:4 by bringing up their children in the training, instruction - and discipline! (NASB) - of the Lord' (p.12) [Dennett's exclamation mark]. This particular verse follows the instruction to children to obey their parents, and is followed by the instruction to slaves to 'obey their earthly masters with fear and trembling, single-mindedly, as serving Christ'.

It is evident that, even if one were to accept the literal authority of the Bible, there are severe difficulties in using it to justify separate Christian schools. Moreover, refutation does not have to rely on any of the findings of Biblical criticism (which would be rejected by those involved). In practice, it is immediately evident that the interpretation of these passage (which are seen as central to most justifications) is highly selective - indeed perverse. Deuteronomy 6 certainly states that God's laws were to be passed on from father to son and, in a largely illiterate society, there was no other way of maintaining a body of known law. The passage clearly indicates that parents were expected to have a central role to play in teaching their children the law. This aspect is taken literally, yet none of the new Christian schools would assume that they should 'bind them as a sign on the hand and wear them as a phylactery on the forehead; write them up on the doorposts of their homes and on their gates', nor do they interpret these laws as only applying to the 'land of milk and honey'. Clearly, this passage has much to say about the way the Israelites believed that God enters history and might be reasonably interpreted to have something to say about the importance of children learning the law of God and even the Christian message, but it says nothing about separate Christian schooling. To stretch its meaning to support separate Christian schools is read it selectively, wrench it out of its context and, at the same time, to invest it with meanings that it could not possibly have held for the Israelites.

Psalm 78 also has nothing direct to say about schooling. Again, it is concerned with the passing on of knowledge about God and the law. Fathers are expected to have this major role with regard to their sons. The interpretation is again highly selective. This passage and Deuteronomy 6 are concerned with passing on knowledge of God and the law to *boys* and Psalm 78 makes it clear that this is the *father's* responsibility. Such sexism is a reflection of the time, but is still followed by ultra-orthodox Jews. Within the new Christian schools, however, while there is still debate about the acceptance of women in leadership roles in the churches and in the schools, the vast majority of teachers are women. The schools are also open to girls as well as boys, and generally there is little difference in the educational (as opposed to social) opportunities open to them.

In Ephesians 6:4 Paul repeats the emphasis on it being the father's responsibility to give instruction and correction. Dennett gives the impression that he would accept the later role, while being prepared to delegate the former responsibility to women. But this verse gives little support for separate Christian schools. Moreover, how is it possible to use this quotation as a justification for Christian schools when it is followed by an instruction to slaves which, far from questioning the legitimacy of slavery, simply states that slaves should obey their 'masters' wholeheartedly as it is the will of God'? I do not believe that any of those involved with the new Christian schools would believe that slavery could be the will of God today, yet they appear to be prepared to quote the preceding verse as if its meaning requires no further investigation or interpretation.

Further difficulties are found with the six brief quotations in the first school prospectus example. Here, however, it is not clear whether the school is trying to justify Christian education as such or the existence of separate Christian schools. At first sight it might appear that the first proverb has little to do with education at all. But on examining this reference it becomes clear that 'The fear of the Lord is the beginning of wisdom' is to be read as just the first phrase of the relevant Biblical reference. It is worth noting that the expectation is that readers of the prospectus will either already know or will check the full references. The first proverb goes on to say 'but fools scorn wisdom and discipline. Attend, my son, to your father's instruction and do not reject the teaching of your mother...' and thus can be interpreted to support the idea that parents are central to the educative process. The second proverb, 'Righteousness exalts a nation', is presumably included for its general message rather than to act as a specific justification for Christian schools.

The third of these proverbs 'Train a child in the way he should go and when he is old he will not turn from it' was a favourite amongst many of the schools. However, the terminology of 'training' was usually used as a Biblical basis for corporal punishment. The New English Bible version of 'Start a boy on the right road, and even in old age he will not leave it' both excludes girls and has none of the associations of punishment.

The quotation from Deuteronomy chapter 6 is particularly interesting as it is used as a key text by Dennett and Van Brummelen as well as being included in this prospectus. The difficulties of applying this text to the present day have already been discussed.

Next come two quotations from the New Testament. 2 Timothy 3, again, can be interpreted to mean that Christian parents should play a very important role in passing on to their children the 'sacred writings which have power to make you wise and lead you to salvation through faith in Jesus Christ' (v 15), while Philippians 4 v 8 is part of Paul's signing-off salutations in his letter and is addressed to all those Christians at Philippi.

In summary, of the six quotations, one seems to have nothing specifically to do with education at all. Two are general instructions about the behaviour of all Jews or the Christians at Philippi. One is used to justify corporal punishment and the other two might be interpreted as saying that Christian parents should have a significant role in teaching their children the Christian message. Most readers would find nothing here that justifies (or even has more than passing relevance to) the idea of separate Christian schools.

Pragmatic justifications for separate schools

It has been argued above that those who claim to be Biblically-based often use the Bible in such a way that 'proof texts' will be interpreted to support their own particular policies and actions. There seems to be an inner demand to find a specific Biblical reference which can then give unambiguous guidelines for living that do not need to be interpreted. In practice, this simple analysis of these books and six quotations reveals that authority within this form of Biblically-based Christianity 'does not really lie with the Bible but with those who claim and have the authority to interpret it' (Maitland, 1992). For outsiders, this use of the Bible to provide 'proof texts' is unconvincing and actually weakens the case that could be made for separate Christian schools. A justification that relies on a broader interpretation of the Bible and the practicalities of providing a Christian environment in current state-maintained schools is much stronger.

It was indicated in the preceding chapter that there were a variety of pragmatic and practical reasons for establishing particular Christian schools. One frequent feature was to counter what were perceived to be negative aspects of the local state-maintained schools. Local schools were either seen as presenting a human-centred philosophy where God and Christianity had no place or one where a variety of religious and superstitious beliefs and practices were encouraged.

Additionally, some parents had been concerned about the academic aspects of schooling, for example large class size, or ineffective teachers. Others reacted to concerns about lack of discipline and moral standards in the schools. As might be expected, religious aspects were central.

The diversity of reasoning is best illustrated through a consideration of some of the interview material that was collected from Headteachers of these new Christian schools during the research. They were asked to describe the events that led to the establishment of their schools and were encouraged to talk at length about the issues that had concerned them about state schools.

So, I moved here in October 1984. Brought my children from a small Church of England school to a very big town infant and Junior school. I was very disturbed by what was going on there. My child was having problems - they weren't severe problems but when I spoke to the Headmistress it was a case of, well there are children with more problems than his, and there's a limit to what we can do, because we have so many children with problems. And then I went to see the Headteacher of the junior school about my daughter's teacher. He just seemed to write endlessly on the board and the children just copied mindlessly, and it seemed so unstimulating and his response was that 'Mr Jones wants to retire, we want him to retire, you are the seventh parent who has complained to me about this, but there is absolutely nothing I can do about it'. So I felt disenchanted, really, that there were problems in the education system, but nobody seemed to be able to do anything about it. And when I spoke to more people, I found that there were others who had been through similar situations - headteachers or teachers really wanting to help, but feeling somehow that they couldn't, they were restrained by other people, people above them or the system or whatever, lack of resources...

g.w. What is interesting about that, I find, is that you are actually talking about the educational aspects that are not concerned with Christianity.

Yes, there were other things that had been niggling away. My seven year old son came home from school one day and said, 'what is LSD?' And I said, well, 'why do you need to know?' And he said that we were doing this thing about the '60s, and Mrs Watson said we were going to do a project on the Beatles, and she was talking about LSD. And I thought there were a lot more edifying things in this world that seven year olds could do a project on rather than the Beatles. So I had to sit down and explain to him that, although the Beatles had been highly acclaimed as significant people in the '60s and early '70s, in fact, they were very misguided and their lives weren't rooted in Christ in a way we would want to applaud people who were following a Godly life, these people were actually very sad and sorry people. And, although Mrs Watson things they're wonderful and marvellous and loves the Beatles and has every record they've ever produced, that doesn't mean they are the sort of people we would like you to find out about (light laugh). So there were things like that disturbed me. There was one incident where I had to go into the infant school to speak to the teacher about the emphasis on other religions. They have two children which, I don't know which religion it is, but they celebrate Divali, but they had two children in the school, so they went overboard on Divali and other such celebrations to the point of actually having an act of worship in the school which my children were expected to take part in. And when I went and made the point that I was happy for them to learn *about* other religions but I don't want them taking part in the actual worship, the teachers just couldn't see the difference, the differentiation, between those two things. And they thought I was mad. So there were those things going on as well. All in all we felt that, as Christians, the Lord has given us very clear guidelines about how to treat people and how to do things in the right way for the right motivation. And we felt we could set up a school and do the job far better than other schools. (I.5)

A second interviewee (quoted in chapter 2) discussed the need to establish a school:

I think the divide between Christian education and state education has become far, far greater over recent years - humanism is taught and not only in the curriculum, but in terms of what children learn in the playground, it is far from what we would want. And I think that is possibly the biggest influence, what children learning the playground. And what they are going to learn there is many times undesirable. We have seen it from children who have come into the school who have been in state schools before, sometimes the attitudes and ideas they bring in, we just say 'no, we don't want that here, it is not what we believe it is how a Christian should act' or whatever. All the while in the state sector these things are being absorbed into their lives.

g.w. what sort of things?

In detail? Rude little jokes, rude words, aggression, even fear. Some of the pupils we have had - one boy was thrown down the stairs. He said that the boys used to wait for him outside the gate to attack him. And they said they could do nothing because it was outside the gate. I don't think that people like us who were at school a long time ago really appreciate what it is like to be honest. So it is the whole atmosphere that is different. We simply say it is a training for life.

While a third described the process:

About five years ago we had one family in the school who began to get a vision for Christian education. They were very unhappy with what was happening to their children in the state system. The fact that they were having a multi-faith education, but more than that, it was a humanistic education. And they began to get a vision for Christian education, which instead of being man-centred or child-centred education was a God-centred education, with Christian values, and basically one that gave a unity from the home and the Church and the school. Instead of which they were putting certain standards and principles into their children at home and these were being reinforced by the church, but they were being undone at school. And positively spoken against, rather than being encouraged. So they had a vision for Christian education, and they took their children out of the state system and educated them at home. They were actually teachers. They would have been 7 and 5 and a 3 year old I think. They continued with that for a year and then some other families that wanted to have Christian education for their children, so they had 10 children the following year. And there was then more and more interest in the Church and the Church took the vision on. It's a house church, we hire halls, and this is our building.

[This county] is quite a left-wing council and some of their policies are very left wing. In fact, at one time it had the worst reputation outside Brent for education. And some of those policies were quite offensive to Christian parents... like the teaching of multi-faith, which I don't really have a problem with. I would tell our children about the Hindus and that kind of thing, but we wouldn't treat it as truth. Whereas everything is celebrated [in this county] - Divali was celebrated, all sorts of things. Halloween was a big issue for a lot of parents. A lot of the syllabuses that they follow had a tremendous amount of stories about witches and that sort of thing that spiritually we would find hard. There was a letter sent round at one stage which said to parents - how is your children's register set out? Is it set out girls first, boys first? Or age? Do your letters come always addressed to Mr and Mrs? Are they ever addressed to Mrs and Mr? And all this kind of thing - which a lot of our parents found offensive. They sound little things but when they are all coming to you like that, it's quite a barrage... So a lot of parents were very keen to come here.

Finally, the headteacher already quoted at the beginning of this chapter explained:

We also object that evolution is taught as a fact and not as a theory. I've been into schools to talk - big secondary schools - and I could have gone in as a minister and 'preached' to them about creation. But I didn't. I went along and said to them, let's be academic about this, I want to give you another theory. I want you to see evolution as a theory, and I want you to see another theory as equally worthy of consideration. I was talking like this, and the science teacher he just shouted out - in front of all the school. He just couldn't be challenged even at that academic level that creation was worthy of study.

g.w. He shouted out that that was untrue?

Yes, oh yes. He wouldn't accept that evolution was a theory. So it is this sort of thing. We are creationists and we present the scientific evidence for creation.

g.w. Are you totally literal about it, six days and so on?

45

Yes, my only question would be, why did God take so long. Yes, of course there are some Christians who go for a gap theory, but we believe it was six days.

And that is our stance for faith. And we believe that is the best foundation to teach about other faiths. Rather than say that these are all the faiths. They all meet in the same way. They all lead to God, all speaking the same etc etc, and making it much of a mish-mash - I think it was Caroline Cox who talked about the mish-mash back in the 1988 debate - with morning worship as well. So we are clearly Christian, but we teach from that Christian stance about evolution and other faiths etc.

The Bible says that we should train up our children in the way they should go. Deuteronomy talks about the Jewish nation - it's a picture for us now - to talk about their laws, to share their laws, to have them written on their foreheads... Their whole lives were to be based on God. So our challenge would be: I don't have to have a special reason to put my children as a father in a Christian school, for I am simply doing what God want me to do - to train the children up - my children - in the way that they should go. Everything is based on God's will.

Now how could I obey that command to train up my children the way they should go when so much of their five day a week schooling is against those standards or at the very least is not based on them?
So for that positive reason I need to put my children in a place where the standards and attitudes and the ethos are in sympathy with what I would teach at home. It is the family, church and school that work together for the child... There are some who argue that Christian children should be in other schools to act as 'light and salt' but young children are not able to deal with some of the academic arguments put forward. A young child would not be able to deal with a convinced evolutionist - it's just not fair to allow that child, or to put that child in that position. They need to develop themselves. Plus the fact that, while this is a Christian school, the children aren't angels - so as far as their own faith and commitment are concerned that's up to them as individuals. That's up to them whether they become Christians or not. So we have children here who are of all ages some of whom have made a commitment and some who haven't... We need

46

to train a soldier before we put them out to war.

So there are very positive ways why the school started. We always share it with parents in terms of two ps. It is protection, but not in a negative sense. All good parents will put the medicines out of the way, they will put the stair-gate on, they will put the safety belts on in the car and then, often, they will let them go to school without any sense of protection. And the second p is preparation. We prepare them to be full citizens in all ways. If they want their faith developing we help them with that, but we clearly try to develop them to at least be aware of all the different debates and standards that they need to be aware of when they leave school.

We are quite happy to work with anybody. That doesn't mean they or we have to compromise. I'd be happy to sit with a Muslim and work on an initiative together, but if we were talking, I would still share with him that I believe that Christ is the only way to the Lord, the only way to the Father, because that is what Jesus said. That wouldn't be asking him to compromise, but I wouldn't want him to ask me to say that all faiths lead to the one God. So, in a democracy, although I would disagree with their faith stance, because I do not believe it will lead to salvation, because I believe that Christ presents it, I still feel that they have a right, as long as they work within the democratic structures of this country and clearly within the law, I can't see how we can stop them having faith schools. I mean why should be have Church of England, Catholic schools, Jewish schools, Methodist schools. And I don't feel that it would lead to ghetto schooling.

The last head interviewed was one of those who had been quite closely involved with the Christian Schools Trust and the Christian Schools Campaign. Clearly, he had thought through his position more thoroughly than the others. It is noticeable that he too quoted from Deuteronomy 6 in defence of separate Christian schools, but does so through analogy rather than as a direct instruction. He was able to summarize many of the reasons for parents and churches wishing to establish separate schools in a way that the others were unable to. Some of these reasons relate to perceived academic and discipline problems in state schools, so that there is a lack of harmony between school and home in the behaviour expected of the child, and a feeling that the schools were failing the child academically. But far more important is the belief that state schools present an anti-Christian belief system to their children. These Heads saw state schools as promoting secular humanism, and devaluing Christianity by presenting all religions as equal. The schools' presentation of a 'multi-cultural mish-mash' was seen by all Heads as a key problem for Christian parents. Some did not wish their children to know anything about other faiths, while others were happy for them to know about them, but believed that these other faiths should be taught as simply incorrect. Nearly all were against any celebration of the festivals associated with other faiths, and all were against their children being asked to participate in worship which involved other faiths. They firmly reject the idea that all faiths lead to one God, and believe that Jesus Christ is the 'only way to God and salvation'.

Here we have evidence of Christians who hold strongly to their evangelical faith and believe that state schools present an anti-Christian message. It is worth remembering that about half of these schools teach primary school age children only, and this is partly because there is particular concern about the teaching received by younger children. It is recognised that, at some point, children must be able to face the reality of a predominantly secular society. There is debate as to whether this should occur as early as eleven, but there is certainty that it is undesirable for it to occur at primary level.

These general argument are far harder to counter than the specific arguments based on selective interpretation of Biblical texts. They actually involve very complex arguments about the balance between the mutual rights of parents, children and the state within a democratic, multi-cultural society.

48

4 Early campaigning

The Campaign for State Support

The Christian Schools Campaign was far from the first pressure group to campaign for state support for particular private schools. Indeed, it might be argued that any history of a campaign for state support for alternative schools must date back to before 1833, for this was the first year in which the British government was persuaded to give financial support to private church organizations to support 'the erection of school houses' (Walford, 1990a). In one way or another, successive governments have continued to give support to various non-government controlled schools since that time. However, there is a range of recent pressure groups that have a closer association with the Campaign that eventually led to support for a range of faith-based schools through the 1993 Education Act.

One particular group worth considering is the Campaign for State Supported Alternative Schools (CSSAS) which was started in December 1979 during an Advisory Centre for Education (ACE) conference. Its aim, according to Laura Diamond (1989) co-founder of CSSAS, was to encourage the establishment of small, democratically-organized, alternative schools funded by the state.

One of the key political figures involved in the campaign was Michael Young, now Lord Young of Dartington. Educated at the progressive Dartington Hall School (of which he has written a biography of the founders (Young, 1983)), Young became an eminent sociologist (see for example: Young and Wilmott, 1957, 1973; Young, 1958; Young and Schuller, 1988) and an outstanding political campaigner on education and consumer issues. Among many other prominent positions he is President of the Consumers' Association, the National Extension College and, the organization of most interest here, the Advisory Centre for Education (ACE). A long time advocate of increased choice in education, Young spoke at an ACE conference in December 1978 about what he saw as the increasing uniformity of education provision within the comprehensive system, and of his fear that parents might feel forced to use the private sector to obtain the diversity of provision that they wished for. As a result of this meeting a small group of parents, teachers and ACE workers developed a document, *A Case for Alternative Schools within the Maintained Sector* (ACE, 1979), which was later adopted as the policy document for the CSSAS.

It is important to note that CSSAS was a narrowly based campaign. It brought together only those people interested in a particular type of alternative school, rather than supporting all the demands for state funding for private education. In the policy document (ACE, 1979) it was made clear that CSSAS supported non-fee-paying schools that were to be non-selective on grounds of ability or aptitude and would not discriminate on grounds of race, sex or religion. It was accepted that it would be necessary to demonstrate sufficient demand for a particular school before state funding was forthcoming, and that HMIs and health and safety inspectors should play a part in ensuring appropriate standards. While admitting that several models were possible, the one advocated was that of a democratic, open, non-hierarchical, non-coercive and non-violent school. In short, the vision of schooling to be supported was that of the progressive free school that had become popular in the 1960s and early 1970s, and which drew upon the child-centred and libertarian education ideas of educationists such as A S Neill, Homer Lane, Dora Russell, John Holt, Neil Postman and others. These ideas had spawned some 20 or 30 small private free schools during that period, organized by parents and teachers anxious to rid themselves of the hierarchical oppressiveness of many state maintained schools (Wright, 1989). These 'new romantics', as Hargreaves (1974) has designated them, had an influence on educational thinking far out of proportion to their numerical strength, but attempts to translate their thinking into the state sector were few and short lived. Michael Duane's Risinghill (Berg, 1968), R F Mackenzie's (1970) Braehead and John Watts' (1980) Countesthorpe College (Gordon, 1986) all came to tragic ends. The private free schools also had limited lifetimes, and by the time of the launch of CSSAS in 1979 only two of the newer free schools survived - Kirkdale School and White Lion Free School. In practice, the campaign had been launched because the free schools were finding it increasingly difficult to support themselves from their own resources, but it had been started too late and the external environment changed too quickly for the campaign to be successful. After some initial success in terms of membership and publicity, by 1982, only a handful of dedicated workers remained, and the last newsletter was published in 1984.

Diamond (1989) analyses the failure of CSSAS in terms of mistakes made within the organization, the difficulty of the task and the changing external environment. She argues that the attack on progressive education led by the Black Papers was an important part of this changed environment (Cox and Dyson, 1971). These right-wing writers had reviled progressive education as lowering educational standards and diverting the schools from their task of training young people for work. At the time of publication, the Black Papers had been largely ignored by most of those involved in education, but by the 1980s the vision of schooling presented by them had become the accepted wisdom of government. Rhodes Boyson (1974), one of the original Black Paper writers and co-editor of the 4th Paper (Cox and Boyson, 1975), was for a time a Minister for Education within the Conservative government. Under such new circumstances, calls for the state to help prop-up ailing free schools sounded somewhat ridiculous.

Diamond (1989:79) also argues that the campaign would have been more likely to have been politically successful if it had included other sorts of alternative schools that did not necessarily fit within the restricted free-school model, for example, the Steiner Schools and the Small School at Hartland. Although not fully following the 'new romantic' model, these schools have many features in common with the model, and might be seen as a more acceptable 1980s version of the original.

The Human Scale Education Movement

The Small School at Hartland in Devon is a unique secondary school founded and organized by a small group of educational activists who retained some of the idealism of the 1960s. The school's founder, Satish Kumar, is Chairman of the Schumacher Society and editor of *Resurgence*, a magazine with a concentration on environmental issues. The school was started in 1982 simply because Kumar had recently moved to Hartland and there was no local secondary school for his children (Winsor, 1987), but it has since become the centre of a wider movement for state supported small schools. In 1989 the school had two full-time teachers on low salaries, 13 part-time staff, and 31 pupils (Blackburne, 1989). The head, Colin Hodgetts, trained as a clergyman, and is former director of Christian Action and coordinator of a programme to resettle Vietnamese refugees in Britain, and sees the school as a continuation of his campaigning career. Together, Kumar and Hodgetts managed to convince charitable foundations such as the Calouste Gulbenkian Foundation and the Sainsbury Family Charitable Trust that the school was worth supporting on an experimental basis, and that it could serve as a basis for future small secondary schools funded by the state. With this in mind, a team of researchers from Exeter University was asked to evaluate the school over a three year period. Their report, published in 1989, argued that the school was providing a full curriculum, that mixed-age teaching was successful, but that the school did have the special benefits of an influx of skilled people who could teach part-time, and that the school had yet to capitalize on all the educational advantages of small schools (Golby et al, 1989). The school applied to the Secretary of State for Education and Science to become established as a voluntary aided non-fee-paying secondary school, but the application was rejected in 1991.

The Schumacher Society, under the chairmanship of Satish Kumar, had decided to develop a movement to spread the Small School model. The Human Scale Education Movement was launched in September 1987 at a conference in Oxford. Much of the work in organising that conference was done by Philip Toogood, previously a controversial head of Madeley Court Comprehensive School in Telford, who was invited to Hartland to teach and coordinate the launch. At Telford, Toogood (1989) had established semi-autonomous mini-schools, each with about 100 pupils, within the 1st to 3rd years of his large comprehensive school. Timetables were blocked into half days, pupils given a territory of their own and parental involvement encouraged. However, after seven years he retired early following conflict with the LEA over how the school was to be run.

These activities led to his appointment at Hartland and to his early work with the Human Scale Education Movement. The Movement has three main initiatives for action and support: minischools, small schools and flexischooling. Minischooling is simply the restructuring of large schools into smaller ones as had been done at Madeley Court. Small-schools are to be encouraged especially where the intention is that they should be free and have open access.

Flexischooling is a way of encouraging schools to combine school-based learning with home-based or community-based education, which developed out of Education Otherwise activities (Meighan, 1988).

In 1987 Toogood moved to become head of Dame Catherine's School in Ticknall, Derbyshire that teaches a small number of children aged 4 to 16. Thanks to an eighteenth century trust, it occupies the village's former primary school, and is able to offer free education to the local community's children, supported by the voluntary fund-raising activities of local parents and villagers. The mixed age learning environment means that teaching is again individualized, but here the emphasis is on developing a high degree of self-reliance and resourcefulness, and on the children learning for themselves 'so that they really own the knowledge that they acquire' (Toogood, 1988). It follows the ideas of flexischooling (Meighan, 1988) where flexibility and diversity in teaching approaches are championed and where the classroom is seen as just one possible location for learning. Some of the children spend only part of the week at the school and are taught by their parents at home for the remainder. The school sees itself as an open learning centre for the children and adults of the local community. Dame Catherine's has also become the base for a regular journal *Education Now* and for a publishing cooperative that links university and college academics with practising teachers and campaigners.

The Human Scale Education Movement (now known more simply as Human Scale Education) has thrived and, by 1992 had an impressive list of Patrons. These included Tim Brighouse (now Director of Education for Birmingham) Sir Yehudi Menuhin, Jonathon Porritt, Professor Richard Pring (University of Oxford), Anita Roddick (Body Shop) and Lord Young of Dartington. It organizes regular conferences (including an international conference at Oxford co-sponsored with the European Foundation for Freedom in Education) and now acts as a pressure group for a variety of interlinked causes. In particular, it wishes to see a greater diversity of small schools receiving state support through a variety of funding arrangements.

The 1988 Education Reform Act

State maintained small schools have fared badly during the tenure of successive Conservative governments. Very few small secondary schools now exist and many small primary schools have been closed because of falling school rolls and economic constraints on local education authorities. While parental support for small schools has generally been high, local and central government have seen them as uneconomic, and unable to offer the quality and diversity of educational experience obtainable in larger schools. On the other hand, and in some conflict, the Conservative government has gradually increased its interest in the idea of extending choice in education, first through the Assisted Places Scheme, and later through open enrolment, grant-maintained schools, and the development of private City Technology Colleges. CTCs gave new impetus to those fighting to obtain state funding for existing alternative private schools. They argued that, if the state could support parents' choice for technological education, why could it also not support parents' choice for a variety of other forms of private education?

The implications and potentials of the CTC initiative and the government's proposals for 'opting-out' were not lost on the new Christian schools. After the Education Reform Bill was published in November 1987, a few of the heads arranged to see Brian (now Lord) Griffiths who was at that time Head of the Prime Minister's Policy Unit. Their hope was that the government itself might add an amendment to the Bill or support amendments that were due to be put forward in the Lords. Lord Griffiths is a firm Anglican who believes that extending choice in education is an essentially Christian activity (Griffiths, 1990). When he met with the heads of these schools, he asked for more information and that a report on the schools be submitted to him. This report was prepared and was later published in a modified form by Ruth Deakin (1989) who, at that time was Headteacher of one of the schools. More important, it would appear that the eventual establishment of a separate pressure group resulted from this meeting with Lord Griffiths, for he accepted that there appeared to be some injustice, but argued that there was a need to generate a campaign before the government could be expected to act. Lord Griffiths believed that it was too late for anything to be included in the 1988 Education Reform Act, but that the schools should look to the longer term and try to change public opinion. The best way forward would be to launch a campaigning organization which would produce news and information on the schools and which would work towards the introduction of a further Bill.

The Heads were aware of forthcoming amendments in the Lords because they already had close contact with Baroness Cox who was one of the proposers of an amendment. Baroness Cox was a key figure in the New Right, and a strong supporter of the new Christian schools. Her contacts with the schools went back several years and she was even the official guest at one of the school's prize days in the mid 1980s. Following an academic background in nursing and sociology, Caroline Cox was made Baroness in 1982, and from 1983 to 1985 was Director of the Right-wing Centre for Policy Studies. She is a committed Anglican and a member of the Franciscan Third Order. She has also been a key member of several small but influential right wing educational groups including the Academic Council for Peace and Freedom, the Educational Research Trust, the National Council for Academic Standards (NCAS) and the Parental Alliance for Choice in Education (PACE) (Griggs, 1989). Significantly, she was a contributor to one of the Black Papers (Cox et al, 1977) and to the Hillgate Group's two influential pamphlets *Whose Schools?* (1986) and *The Reform of British Education* (1987). She is also firmly in favour of selective schooling (Marks et al, 1983, Cox and Marks, 1988).

The two Hillgate pamphlets with which Baroness Cox was involved are prime examples of the writings of the neo-conservative wing of the New Right identified by such critics as Ball (1990a). The main thrust is a strident attack on local education authorities, some of which are seen as being responsible for 'corrupting the minds and souls of the young' through anti-sexist, anti-racist and anti-heterosexist initiatives. A strong 'back to basics' movement is encouraged about curriculum, selective admissions policies advocated for popular schools and a greater diversity of schools receiving funding directly from central government is proposed.

> The aim, we believe, is to offer an independent education to all, by granting to all parents the power, at present enjoyed by only the wealthy, to choose the best available education for their children. This aim can be accomplished only by offering schools the opportunity to liberate themselves from Local Authority control. (Hillgate Group, 1987: 1)

It was almost inevitable that attempts to persuade the government to extend the CTC model to include other types of alternative private schools would be made in Parliament as the Education Reform Bill was passing its way through both Houses. As with many of the successful amendments, the action took place in the Lords rather than the Commons, with somewhat similar amendments being proposed by Lord Young of Dartington and Baroness Cox of Queensbury. On 16 May 1988, at the Committee stage (Hansard, 497, 38-41), Lord Young moved his amendment 230 entitled 'New foundation schools. Extension of parental choice.' The vision of educational choice presented here was far wider than that of the Campaign for State Supported Alternative Schools of a decade earlier. State funding was sought for schools that would vary in respect of educational principle, size of school, curricula emphasis, method of teaching, and particular faith of philosophy espoused. The free school was now just one of a variety of models that were to be supported, but some of the former idealism was still to be detected in the demands that the schools should be academically comprehensive, open without discrimination to all children in their catchment areas, and that the schools should admit children on the basis of criteria compatible with the practice of their local authority if they could not accept all applicants. A further restriction was that they were not 'to propagate doctrines tending to foment racial, religious or other forms of intolerance', but Young made it clear in his speech that his amendment included the possibility of Hindu, Muslim and Buddhist schools to supplement existing denominational schools. He elaborated the example of Denmark, where he claimed that there are no fee-paying schools, as all types of school are state supported. In fact, about eight per cent of pupils in Denmark attend private schools and, as government support is up to a maximum of 85 per cent of the school's expenditure, most of these pupils do pay fees (Doyle, 1989). While these fees are generally small, some are substantial (Mason, 1989) which means that, even though some free places are available to children from low income families, there remains a barrier between the state and private sectors in Denmark.

In the Lords' debate, Baroness Cox suggested that the route to greater diversity and choice in schooling was to make it easier for private schools to attain voluntary aided status. She was particularly concerned about the number of small schools which had tried unsuccessfully to obtain such status over several years. In her supporting speech she explicitly mentioned the Yesodey Hatorah Jewish school, the John Loughborough Seventh Day Adventist school in Tottenham and the 'many other Christian and Muslim schools which are mushrooming in various parts of the country' (Hansard, 497, 43). She argued that all of these schools were supported by parents, often at great personal cost and sacrifice, because they were dissatisfied with local authority schools, and that the Secretary of State for Education and Science should be given extra powers to grant voluntary aided status against the advice of LEAs.

These amendments thus maintained the attack on Local Education Authorities and worked towards the long-term aim of a system of diverse independently run schools. Caroline Cox and others on the political right with similar aims (for example, Sir Rhodes Boyson and Stuart Sexton) actively supported a variety of new small schools in the name of parental choice, and claimed that the existence of these schools was an indicator of growing dissatisfaction with LEA provision. Diversity was encouraged, and opting out of LEA schools into schools that cater for idiosyncratic parental demands was presented as a positive response to the perceived shortcomings of the state system.

There were clear differences in emphasis between Lord Young and Baroness Cox in their presentations as well as in their favoured solution to the problem of increasing state support for a variety of schools. This was noticed by Lord Peston who claimed that the two amendments were fundamentally different - one being about openness and the common school working on comprehensive principles, which he could support, and the other about narrow doctrinaire schools which he could not. In reply, however, both Lord Young and Baroness Cox glossed over these differences, with Young making it clear that his amendment would include religious schools of various denominations.

Baroness Hooper, on behalf of the government, argued that the new schools proposed by Lord Young were unlikely to be able to provide a broad and balanced curriculum, and explained that it was open to such schools that could do so to apply for voluntary aided status. She stated that the amendment would not be timely for inclusion within the 1988 Act, but added that this did not mean that 'the idea will be lost for all time'. Lord Young's amendment was withdrawn, Baroness Cox's not moved, and the campaigners regrouped for a new onslaught at a later date.

The Christian Schools Campaign

It was not until after the 1988 Education Reform Act had become law that the heads of the new Christian schools finally acted to set up the campaigning organisation that had been suggested at the earlier meeting with Brian Griffiths. In consequence, at the beginning of 1989 the Christian Schools Campaign was established with the long term goal of obtaining public funding for the schools (CSC, 1989). The Campaign was linked to the Christian Schools Trust in terms of some overlaps in office holders, but legally separate from the charitable Trust so that it could engage in political activities. When the Christian Schools Campaign was formed 47 schools were involved, at least 13 of which had made unsuccessful initial applications to their LEAs for voluntary aided status.

The Campaign was established with a Director (Ruth Deakin, who was headteacher of a large school in Bristol), a Steering Committee of six (most of whom were also heads of large new Christian schools) and, as had been suggested at the initial meeting with Brian Griffiths, an impressive list of well-known and influential people of various political persuasions who were to act as Patrons. These Patrons were intended to give the Campaign a higher public and political profile, and included among the eleven Lord Young of Dartington, Baroness Cox of Queensbury, Viscount Tonypandy, Anthony Coombs MP, Michael Alison MP, Frank Field, MP, Professor David Regan, Charles Martin, and the Rt Rev Dr George Carey. It was an impressive, and 'politically balanced' list of supporters, and had been obtained largely through private correspondence. Some of Patrons had agreed to become Patrons without even meeting the Heads of any of the schools, let alone seeing any of the schools in operation! As discussed more fully in chapter 7, George Carey was clearly one of the Patrons who was not fully knowledgeable about the Campaign. At the time of agreeing to be Patron, George Carey was Bishop of Bath and Wells (the Diocese in which the Campaign had started), but was translated to the Arch-bishopric of Canterbury in 1990. In September 1991 he gave a speech to the Anglican Secondary School Heads that was interpreted by the press as including an attack on the new Christian schools. Under headlines such as 'Dr Carey turns on his own campaign' (Lodge, 1991b), Carey was reported as saying that some Christian schools were 'socially divisive, educationally damaging and spiritually unsatisfying'. After a meeting with the somewhat astonished Director of the Campaign, he resigned as Patron.

The range of Patrons willing to support the Campaign shows that it is not possible to simply equate the Campaign with the New Right. However, it is true that the most active political Patrons have been the Right wing conservative members - Michael Alison in the House of Commons and Baroness Cox in the House of Lords. Both of these have played very important roles in pushing for legislation on a range of moral and Christian issues such as pornography, religious education and sex education in schools (see, for example, Durham, 1992, and Alison and Edwards, 1990), and played an important part in the passage of legislation in connection with the new Christian schools.

Muslim pressure groups

A further, and very significant, group pushing for state funding of a variety of schools are those involved with Muslim education. Muslims now form the largest religious minority in Britain. It is estimated that there are about two million nominal adherents to the faith, most of whom are immigrants or descended from immigrants who came to Britain in the 1950s and 1960s from Malaysia, the Middle East, Africa, Bangladesh and India (Dooley, 1991). The nature of immigration led to geographical concentration of Muslims, such that the majority settled in the major urban conurbations.

As the number of Muslim children in Britain gradually increased, so did the calls from some Muslim groups for separate Muslim schools. This desire had many and complex roots, but the most important source was a reaction to the schooling provided by the state for Muslim children. In the 1950s and early 1960s little thought was given to the specific needs of Muslim children. The expectation was simply that immigrant children and their parents should 'integrate' into British society, and when policy first developed it was within a specifically 'assimilationist' framework. Schools were seen as the major site for the future integration of ethnic minority populations.

By the mid 1960s, however, it began to be recognised that such a policy was both undesirable and unlikely to be successful. Government began to talk of a 'multi-cultural' society and multi-cultural education emerged. The desirability of a multi-cultural curriculum was voiced in a Green Paper of 1977, and the idea gradually strengthened to find its strongest advocacy in the Swann Committee's *Education for All* (DES, 1985b). Following concerns about the perceived 'underachievement' of ethnic minority pupils, Swann proposed what he regarded as a reorientation of the educational system to serve a multi-cultural society. The aim of multi-cultural education was to provide a curriculum that reflected the diverse cultural backgrounds of the pupils, and where these cultures were, in principle, equally valued. It meant a broadening of the materials used in schools to include a wider variety of geographical and cultural backgrounds to be studied in English literature. It encouraged a wider study of geography and history beyond the British Isles and, central to the argument here, it favoured a multi-faith approach to religious education.

At one level, a multi-faith approach to religious education could be seen as beneficial. It meant that all children were taught the main features of a variety of religious beliefs, but the approach was usually one of examining the history, doctrines, and official practices of each religion in turn. There was little acknowledgement that faith could be a living reality for adherents or that belief might structure the way in which different people lived. All religions were treated as having a similar status and were to be examined as phenomena. This way of treating religious belief is anathema to many of those who hold to their own belief most strongly. To many followers of Islam, as of other faiths, belief entails denial of the validity of other faiths. Religions are not seen as simply a matter of choice between a variety of similar, and equally valid, alternatives.

A further aspect is that Islam, in particular, is a faith that permeates all aspects of everyday life. It defines what is appropriate dress, food, cleanliness and behaviour, as well as demanding regular worship at specified times during the day. In most state schools little has been done to take account of the special needs of Muslim pupils. Dress has been a particular problem. For women, specified dress includes a *shalwar-quamis* (trousers and pinafore) and a *chador* (headscarf) for secondary pupils. There have been numerous cases of Muslim girls being refused permission to wear either of both of these garments as they are perceived to be against particular schools' uniform regulations. The *chador* has sometimes been said to be a safety danger in science and PE lessons. Some of the Muslim times for prayer fall within school time so, ideally, there might be the provision of a prayer room and a timetable that allows for these breaks. In practice, prayer rooms are rare and even the provision of a place within the school in which prayers could be said is unusual. There have been cases where headteachers who have refused to make any provision have sent Muslim children home for praying in the car park (Dooley, 1991).

This lack of special provision for Muslim pupils in state schools is one of the reasons for the growth in private Muslim schools in Britain. There are clear parallels here between the new Christian schools and the Muslim schools, for where parents take a more fundamentalist view about their beliefs, they wish to have schools where their religious practices are taken seriously. But there are additional reasons for certain Muslim groups to desire separate schools, in particular, racism and perceptions of racism within state schools. For example, the so-called 'Honeyford Affair', where a Bradford headteacher wrote a series of articles critical of multi-cultural education, acted to increase support for separate Muslim schools in Bradford, and also led to increased radicalization of local young Muslim men in particular (Dwyer, 1993). Additionally, the anti-Muslim sentiments inspired by the Salman Rushdie case also led to greater polarization and politicisation around issues of identity for Muslims in Britain.

An additional issue is the desire for separate secondary education for girls. Many Muslims see it as important that older Muslim girls are not taught in the same classes as boys. This particular issue is one that has led some commentators to see the demands for separate schools more in terms of the desires of Muslim men to control the lives of women than to improve their children's schooling (Khanum, 1992). However, while male dominance cannot be ignored, the issue is not simply one of male control, and there is growing evidence for considerable parental support for education for both boys and girls from Muslim parents. Indeed, Halstead (1991) has argued that Muslims calling for single sex schools have much in common with some feminists who argue for the advantages of separation.

It is also important to recognise that Muslims hold a variety of views on the desirability of establishing separate schools. Some parents believe that their children are better served within schools that cater for children with all beliefs and none, while others are content for their children to attend such schools as long as they also attend a supplementary school to teach Islamic law and culture. Those with more fundamentalist beliefs have gradually established private schools and about 28 private Muslim schools are now in operation in Britain. These schools show a considerable range in size, style and facilities (Dooley, 1991). At one extreme is the King Fahad Academy in London, which is very well funded by Saudi Arabia and was founded to cater for the children of Saudi diplomats. At the other extreme are several small schools housed in converted houses with cramped accommodation and few facilities.

The growing emphasis on choice during 1980s led some Muslim campaigning groups to become increasingly vocal in their demands for state funding for such private Muslim schools, and several schools applied for voluntary aided status. For example, Islamia Primary School first applied to Brent in 1986, while Zakaria Girls' School in Batley, Yorkshire applied to Kirklees in 1987. In all cases the requests for state funding have been denied. There have been problems with planning permission, arguments that they were too small to be viable and the reluctance of successive Secretaries of State to agree to new schools, especially Muslim schools which were likely to serve specific ethnic minorities alone, while there were surplus places in other nearby schools. One of the most recent cases was Feversham College in Bradford, formerly the Muslim Girls' Community School, which had support from its local education authority, but whose application was turned down by the Secretary of State in February 1995. According to the Department for Education, the problem was that the school needed to improve its management structure, make its premises safer, and show that it could teach the full National Curriculum. However, a spokesman for the Association of Muslim Schools, Ibrahim Hewitt, was reported as saying that he believed the decision was a political one rather than one based on substantive problems with the school (Pyke, 1995).

As will be shown in the next chapter, a variety of Muslim pressure groups played a part in early campaigns. However in February 1989 a fatwa was imposed on Salman Rushdie which, along with the later Gulf War, made it politically inexpedient for Muslim groups to continue to take a high profile in further campaigns. Additionally, the imposition of the National Curriculum through the 1988 Education reform Act made the possibility of voluntary aided or grant-maintained status less desirable for some Muslim groups. The impact of the National Curriculum also made state funding less desirable for some of the more liberal groups campaigning for state funding. This meant that from 1989 until about 1992, apart from the New Right, the most important group still pushing for new forms of state support was the Christian Schools Campaign.

The Muslim campaign for state support for their schools revived again during 1992 with the publication of the 'White Paper on Muslim Education in Great Britain' by the so-called Muslim Parliament of Great Britain (1992). The Muslim Parliament of Great Britain has no official Government status, but is actually a form of pressure group on behalf of some sections of the Muslim population. The document 'White Paper' presented a review of perceived problems and a 'blueprint for Islamic educational development for the next thirty years'. It includes discussion of a wide range of educational issues, including proposals for an Islamic Open University, a consideration of the role of the Mosque and the issue of supplementary schools, but a central chapter deals with state funding of Muslim schools. This chapter is particularly interesting because it discusses two different ways of achieving the aim. The first is through existing private schools becoming grant-maintained or voluntary aided schools, but the second recognises that it is also possible to produce Muslim schools through existing local authority schools with a high percentage of Muslim children becoming grant-maintained. Indeed, with the extended powers given to governors in the 1988 Education Reform Act, any school may, in practice, give high priority to features of school life that are congruent with a Muslim world view. Technically, they may not be Muslim schools but, if enough of the governors are Muslim, the culture of the school can become Muslim. The long and complicated confrontation between the Headteacher and governors of Stratford school in East

London was linked to an attempt of this type where Muslim governors tried to impose their own view of education on the school.

By 1992 a variety of other Muslim groups had joined the debate about state support for Muslim schools, and the Government's policy for *Choice and Diversity* (DFE, 1992) in state education encouraged them to voice their views. A well-argued example of a response to the Government's White Paper was that produced by the Muslim Educational Trust (1992). This document responded to perceived problems in the National Curriculum, in Religious Education and restated the problems that Muslim schools had experienced in trying to obtain voluntary aided status. It hoped that it would be possible for Muslim schools to be established as grant-maintained without having to first obtain voluntary aided status.

Such publications from Muslim pressure groups came late in the overall campaign. As will be shown in the next chapter, the Christian Schools Campaign were active throughout the period and had considerable influence on public and parliamentary opinion through interventions in the House of Lords.

5 Baroness Cox's Education Bill

Building support

Lord Young and Baroness Cox's attempts to introduce clauses into the 1988 Education Reform Act that would have allowed private schools to 'opt in' was unsuccessful. But the attempt achieved considerable media coverage and made the possibility of such a development in the future more conceivable. Even before the Christian Schools Campaign was officially formed, the momentum was maintained through a series of meetings. One of the first of these meetings consisted of little more than a media event staged for the slack news period following the New Year. On 8 January 1989, a total of about 30 people gathered in John Loughborough School, Tottenham to hear Sir Rhodes Boyson and a variety of other speakers representing a diverse range of schools and educational organizations. The meeting was organized by Gerald Smith who is head of St Peter's Independent School, Northampton, but it was actually a mouthpiece for Sir Rhodes Boyson, who argued for support for private schools as a step towards 'full-blooded privatisation of our schools'. At this meeting partial support from government for fee-paying schools was considered as well as full support for non fee-paying schools. Speakers included Philip Toogood, who was representing the Campaign for Educational Choice, K Davidson, Headmaster of the Seventh Day Adventist John Loughborough School, and Nazar Mustafa, Chairman of the Muslim Education Coordinating Council. For such a small meeting it received remarkable media attention with articles in The Times Educational Supplement and many national newspapers.

Many of these same speakers, including Baroness Cox, Sir Rhodes

Boyson, Nazar Mustafa, Gerald Smith and Ruth Deakin, were also speakers in favour of state support for private schools at a further meeting in mid-April 1989. This April meeting was arranged by the Centre for Educational Choice, a new body established by Lord Young, with the aim to 'explore ways in which a range of non fee-paying schools can be included in the maintained sector'. Partial support by government for fee-paying schools was thus excluded from consideration, and the main emphasis of the discussion was on trying to clarify and ease procedures for new schools to become Voluntary Aided Schools. The public meeting was put forward as a time for discussion prior to a delegation going to the Department of Education and Science to put its case later in the afternoon. This delegation consisted of Sahib Bleher (Muslim Education Services), Ruth Deakin (Christian Schools Campaigns), Colin Hodgetts (Human Scale Education Movement), Prof Sig Prais (Jewish Educationist), Baroness Cox and Lord Young, all of whom had earlier addressed the meeting at Westminster Hall. The meeting was given further academic legitimacy through two other speakers - Roland Meighan from the University of Birmingham (heavily involved in Education Otherwise) and Les Bell from the Open University who talked on Danish schooling, but these, and some other speakers, did not go on the Department of Education and Science.

The delegation was treated with considerable respect, for it was met by Kenneth Baker (then Secretary of State for Education and Science), Angela Rumbold (Minister of State), Robert Jackson (Parliamentary Under-Secretary of State), and nine senior DES officials. It is doubtful if they were told that the whole meeting at Westminster Hall had numbered only about 150, including a contingent of children from Dame Catherine's School! However, raw numbers of supporters are clearly less important than the media attention that can be generated, and small articles subsequently appeared in many of the national papers.

A subsequent report on the meeting at the DES stated that Kenneth Baker had told the delegation that there was no animus in the Department towards new applications for voluntary aided status. It was said that nothing is taken into account except the educational merits or demerits of the case put forward. In practice, however, the attainment of Voluntary Aided Status is unlikely without the support of the relevant local education authority, and only about a month earlier the Association of Metropolitan Councils had unanimously passed a resolution against the establishment of any further voluntary aided schools. This path to public support for small private schools is not as open as it might be.

Writing the Bill

The Christian Schools Campaign played a major part in producing a Private Member's Bill that was eventually introduced into the House of Lords by Baroness Cox in November 1990 and debated in March 1991. The Bill sought to amend the 1988 Act such that certain categories of independent school would be eligible to apply for grant maintained status. It also aimed to amend the 1980 Act to make it easier for independent schools to obtain voluntary aided status against the wishes of the relevant LEA.

The centrality of the position of the Christian Schools Campaign in this Bill can be seen from the wording of the Bill and the way in which that wording was developed. One of the meetings at which pressure group tactics and the wording of the Bill was discussed was held in a Committee Room of the House of Lords on 18 June, 1990. The room was booked by Baroness Cox, and she chaired a meeting of about 20 interested people. Among these present were those involved with the Small Schools Movement, such a Philip Toogood, and others from the Seventh Day Adventist John Loughborough School, the Waldorf Steiner Schools, and MENSA. Also present were Professor Sig Prais, John Marks, Stuart Sexton, Lord Lorderdale, four representatives from the Christian Schools Campaign and two Muslims, Nasa Mustafa from the Muslim Education Coordinating Council and Ibrahim Hewitt from the Islamia Schools Trust. The author attended as an observer.

The discussion at that meeting was opened by Baroness Cox and there were initial contributions from several others. The proposed Bill was then presented to the group by Stuart Sexton, who had drafted it in conjunction with representatives from the Christian Schools Campaign. Stuart Sexton had been policy advisor to two past Conservative Secretaries of State for Education and Science (Mark Carlisle and Keith Joseph), and had been the guiding hand behind the controversial Assisted Places Scheme which gave state funding to encourage academically able children to leave the state maintained sector and move into the private sector. He was later a leading proponent of City Technology Colleges (Walford and Miller, 1991; Whitty et al, 1993), and has been a key figure in the Institute of Economic Affairs and former-Director of its Education Unit. Sexton can be seen as an advocate of the neo-liberal wing of the New Right (Ball, 1990a: 43), yet on the issue of funding for new schools there is strong agreement with the neo-conservative advocates. Over the years Sexton (1987, 1992) has made clear his desire for a fully privatized educational system, preferably financed through vouchers that can be 'topped-up' by parents. In 1987 he set out his 'step-by-step' approach to the eventual introduction of a "market system", a system truly based upon the supremacy of parental choice, the supremacy of purchasing power' (Sexton, 1987: 11). His ultimate plan is to have 'per-capita' funding from the state which would be the minimum sum to be spent on each child's education. This minimum sum would be put towards the costs of schooling at any state maintained or private school. Schools would be allowed to make additional charges to cover any extra provision beyond the basic level of schooling and, as a result, the present sharp distinction between maintained and private schooling would fade away. Further, he envisages that eventually the proportion of taxpayers' money spent on education would reduce from its present level as parents pay more and more for the schooling of their own children. Part of this vision is that the establishment of new private schools would be encouraged through the availability of per capita funding.

> The net effect of all this will be a form of 'privatization', the proportion of which will *not* depend upon the Government of the day but upon 'market forces' and will vary from one part of the country to another depending entirely on the wishes of local parents and the quality of existing local authority provision (Sexton, 1987: 40).

Sexton's involvement in drafting this Bill for Caroline Cox and the Christian Schools Campaign must be seen as a step towards this long-term goal. At the meeting he made it clear that there were two possible reasons for presenting a Bill in the House of Lords. The first was simply to air ideas and to debate, while the second was to produce actual legislative change. He argued that his intention was that this was to be an attempt at the second. This meant that the Bill would have to be simple and straightforward to have a better chance of success, and that it should aim not to be controversial. While not all of those present shared Sexton's belief that the Bill actually had a chance of becoming law, the Bill was certainly drafted with this intention.

The proposals were in two parts. The first dealt with changes to the 1988 Education Reform Act. Here, changes were put forward which would include independent schools alongside county and voluntary schools as being eligible for grant-maintained status. These clauses were carefully drafted such that not all independent schools were to be given this possibility, for the purpose was not to open grant-maintained status for all independent schools, but just for selected schools that 'needed' state support.

Thus, the Bill read that:

The following subsection shall be inserted after subsection (7) of Section 52:-

(7A) The Secretary of State shall by order designate categories of independent schools which shall be eligible to apply for grant maintained status. He shall include in such categories of schools, those which provide an alternative ethos to the existing local maintained schools, including schools with a specifically Christian ethos.

Additionally, another subsection was to be added after subsection (9) of Section 52 of the Education Reform Act that read:

(9A) An independent school is not eligible for grant maintained status if, in the opinion of the Secretary of State, it is already well-endowed financially and has, and is likely to continue to have, adequate private income.

The Bill also sought to amend the 1980 Education Act such that it was easier for schools seeking voluntary aided status to do so. After subsection (4) of Section 13 of the Act was to be added:

The Secretary of State shall approve proposals submitted under this section where the maintaining local education authority objects, provided that all other conditions are met to the satisfaction of the Secretary of State. A surplus of places in other local maintained schools shall not be a sufficient reason for rejection of the proposals. In considering proposals for approval, the Secretary of State shall take into account the need for a diversity of schools within the maintained sector in order to satisfy parental demand and children's needs.

This second part of the Bill sought to make it more difficult for Secretaries of State to reject applications for voluntary aided status by removing the criterion that had been so commonly used by local education authorities and by the Secretary of State. The idea that there was a 'need for diversity' of schools within the maintained sector is also worthy of note, for this Bill was drafted about two years before *Choice and Diversity* (DES, 1992).

The strategy embodied in these proposals was set out in some accompanying 'Speaking Notes to Private Members Bill', and is worth considering in detail as it indicates the seriousness of the attempt to change legislation at this point. While Sexton's long term aim was a fully privatized system, and one where all schools would be treated equally by the state, this Bill was aimed to help those schools 'which cater for families who would normally expect to use the State system of education, but who seek a less secular environment to that found within the usual State school'. Most of the schools the Bill was particularly designed to help were said to have been recently founded and by parents who could not afford the traditional independent schools. Mention is made of the 'great personal hardship' that many parents have encountered in order to establish these schools and of the idea that many of these schools 'offer a well-disciplined Christian environment which I am sure their lordships would welcome'.

It is of note that neither the Bill itself nor the 'Speaking Notes' referred to Muslim schools. In the 'Speaking Notes' the black Seventh Day Adventist John Loughborough school was given as an example of a school that might benefit, as were the orthodox Jewish schools in London, several of which had made unsuccessful applications to become voluntary aided. At the meeting it was argued that the Bill had a much greater chance of success if it only mentioned the possibility of Christian schools, and it was explicitly stated that the promoters did not wish to mention Muslim schools by name. At the same time, it was made clear that the Bill would not exclude the possibility of schools for other faiths in practice. One of the Muslim representatives at the meeting did, however, strongly suggest that the term 'alternative ethos' was too vague and that it would be better if the phrase 'religious ethos' was used. A compromise suggestion, that was accepted, was that the phrase 'religious or philosophical ethos' would be used. This, it was argued, had the advantage of being the phrasing used within the European Convention on Human Rights, which the UK signed in 1950. And indeed, Article 2 of the first Protocol to the Convention states:

No person shall be denied the right to education. In the exercise of any functions which it assumes in relation to education and to teaching, the

State shall respect the right of parents to ensure such education and teaching in conformity with their own religious and philosophical convictions. (Quoted in Lester and Pannick, 1987.)

Such phrasing was thus unlikely to be questioned. One of the Muslim representatives was still unhappy with this wording, and felt that Muslim schools should be explicitly mentioned. In practice, this was ignored and the final wording became:

(7A) The Secretary of State shall by order designate categories of independent schools which shall be eligible to apply for grant maintained status. He shall include in such categories of schools, those which provide an alternative religious or philosophical ethos, including a specifically Christian ethos, to the existing local maintained schools.

For the Bill to have any chance of success it had to be seen to not represent any substantial increase in public expenditure. The second part of the Bill concerned with grant-maintained status attempted to ensure that it would not be possible for the well established and well know private schools to seek grant-maintained status. In particular, it was recognised that if some of the ex-direct grant schools wished to cease being private schools and become grant-maintained, this would entail considerable extra expenditure. The Bill would have little hope of success if it allowed such a change, so the new subsection 9A, attempted to restrict the schools eligible to those that were poorly financed and largely parent-created. The only change made to this subsection was the replacement of 'and' by 'or'. It was suggested and accepted that logically the restriction should exclude those schools which were 'already well endowed financially *or* has, and is likely to continue to have, adequate private income', rather than '*and* has...'

The second part of the Bill tried to make it easier for schools to become voluntary aided by requiring the Secretary if State to ignore the local education authority's objections if all other conditions were met. It also proposed that surplus places in existing maintained schools should not be seen as a valid reason for not granting voluntary aided status. These places were surplus, it was argued, because they had been rejected by parents who had started their own schools instead. The solution was to close the schools that offered places that parents did not want. In the final Bill put before the House of Lords that section was reworded as:

4(A) Notwithstanding subsection (4) above, the Secretary of State may approve proposals submitted under this section even where the maintaining local education authority objects, and in making his decision he shall take into account the need for a diversity of schools within the maintained sector in a particular area in order to satisfy parental demand and children's needs.

4(B) A surplus of places in other local maintained schools shall not in itself be a sufficient reason for the rejection of the proposals by the Secretary of State, and the Secretary of State may direct the local education authority to reduce any surplus of places in its maintained schools and may direct that such surplus places shall be made available for a proposed voluntary school.

At the meeting on 18 June 1990, after the wording of the Bill had been discussed, future strategy was outlined. Several of those with political experience stressed that, while the Bill had been written by Sexton for the Christian Schools Campaign, it was not a good idea to present it as such. It was to be seen as Baroness Cox's Bill, and one that would be co-sponsored by Lord Grimond of Firth (Liberal Democrat) and Lord Young of Dartington (Labour). It was suggested that the various groups should not form an overarching or coalition, but should wait until the Bill was published and then be seen to support it. Lobbying should be done on an individual basis with each group contacting its own supporters and constituencies. It was suggested than once the Bill was published particular sections of the media should be lobbied, and individuals should make personal appointments to see strategically important people.

It is important to recognise the extent of the work that had already been done by the Christian Schools Campaign at this point. The plan was for Baroness Cox to hold a Press Conference on 4 July 1990 in the House of Lords at which the contents of the Bill would be made public. Clearly the Bill had a greater chance of success if a large number of Peers had already said that they supported it, so lobbying of Peers was essential. It was expected that the brief and formal First Reading of the Bill could be in October, which meant that, with the Summer recess, lobbying had to be done in July. The Christian Schools Campaign had already started to build a list of Peers likely to support the Bill, and asked for further help with this activity.

At the meeting it was decided that the Christian Schools Campaign would construct a Press Release about the Press Conference and issue it on behalf of Baroness Cox. In the event, the Press Release of 27 June went out under the Christian Schools Campaign letterhead, and included the Muslim Islamia Primary School as one of several named schools that might benefit from the Bill. The inclusion of a named Muslim school in the Press Release is an indication of the CSC's desire for complete honesty, even where this might be tactically inadvisable. The Press Conference was duly held on 4 July, and resulted in good coverage in the educational press and some articles in national newspapers.

In some ways, however, the Press Conference was a non-event, as Sahib Bleher, Secretary of the Islamic Party of Great Britain and Secretary of Muslim Educational Services, had released the provisional contents of the Bill in early June. Bleher had received copies of the first draft of the Bill, and the government's refusal to grant Islamia Primary School voluntary aided status in May 1990 had led to publicity in which sections of the first draft had been given to the press (Lodge, 1990). In addition, just prior to the Press Conference the Adam Smith Institute gained publicity (Hackett, 1990) about a document that was then at the draft stage which called for parents to be able to establish their own schools. This document was eventually published in 1992 (Pirie, 1992). All this was, of course, extra publicity for the future Bill.

It was believed that for the Bill to have any chance of success in the House of Lords, and then later in the House of Commons, there would need to be consultation with the Secretary of State for Education and Science. However, Kenneth Baker had been replaced as Secretary of State by John MacGregor in July 1989. This change meant that he was still relatively new to the office, and consultation delayed the First Reading. This finally occurred on 12 November 1990, only just before Margaret Thatcher's resignation and a further Cabinet reshuffle brought Kenneth Clarke into office as Secretary of State on 29 November 1990. The new consultation further delayed the date of the debate, it was delayed again because some Tory Peers could not attend a scheduled date and then, once again, to allow for some Labour Peers to attend. The Bill was finally debated on 4 March 1991.

In the eight intervening months the Christian Schools Campaign had written twice to every Member of Parliament, and to about 80 selected Peers. The three central members of the Campaign had also visited about 30 Peers to try to persuade them to support the Bill. They had also addressed the Tory backbench committee on education, discussed the Bill with officials in the Church of England, and talked to many others involved with education. But the delays to the debate led to a new strategy when the Bill was actually put forward.

The debate

By the time of the debate in March 1991 the political situation had changed. Even if the Bill gained approval in the House of Lords, it was expected that a forthcoming General Election (eventually held in April 1992) would ensure that there was no time for it to be passed in the House of Commons. There was very little chance of the Bill becoming law so, what had started as a determined attempt to legislate, became simply another opportunity to raise the issues and level of awareness.

Very unusually, at the start of her opening speech of the debate, Baroness Cox told the assembled Peers that she intended to withdraw the motion at the end of the debate without pressing for a vote. This tactic caused some controversy, for within the House of Lords there are separate procedures for raising a debate and moving a Second Reading. Baroness Cox was later forced to state that, in doing so, she had adopted the advice of 'my seniors and betters, given through the usual channels' who had asked her to withdraw the motion. In fact, the position had become complex. There had been criticism of the wording of the Bill from some of those who supported the general principles. It was argued that the Bill was not sufficiently clear about which independent schools could actually apply for grant-maintained status. Some were concerned that the wording should explicitly include the possibility of some existing special schools being able to apply. Both of these issues were important, but there was also clear evidence that the Bill might not achieve a majority in the House of Lords. More significantly, it appeared that several of the 24 Bishops of the Church of England who sit in the House of Lords were likely to reject the motion. The Rt Rev Michael Adie, Bishop of Guildford and chairman of the Church of England Board of Education had publicly made it clear that, while the Board was generally not against extending aided status to a wider variety of faith-based schools, it did not believe that this required any change in legislation. Neither was it in favour of changes to allow new forms of grant-maintained schools (Lodge, 1991b). More important, according to Geoffrey Duncan, General Secretary of the Board, the Board felt that change was best achieved by exploring with the Secretary of State the ways in which the current law was interpreted. If there was to be legislative change, this was best achieved through proposals brought by one of the major political parties, rather than a Private Member's Bill. With the possibility of a defeat facing the Bill, it was decided to withdraw rather than force a vote. While it was thought that a negative vote would be damaging to the cause, a debate of the issues was still seen as positive.

In her speech, Baroness Cox presented the Bill as having cross-party and cross-faith support. She regretted the unavoidable absence of several supporters such as the former Archbishop of Canterbury, Lord Cogan, and also Lord Jakobovits, the Chief Rabbi. She then described the variety of schools that she wished to see helped through the Bill, and listed some of the groups giving support - the Christian Schools Campaign, the Small Schools Movement, Mensa, the Steiner Fellowship, the Muslim Education Co-ordinating Council, and the Islamic Academy.

In this speech Baroness Cox approached the issue of Muslim schools face-on. In the time since the Bill had been written Iraq had invaded Kuwait, and the whole issue of fundamentalist Islam had come into such prominence that it was no longer possible to ignore the issue of Muslim schools. While the Bill had been framed in such a way that Muslim schools were explicitly not mentioned, they would be undoubtedly one of the foci of the debate. She said:

> This brings me into an area of great controversy. I wish to address the issue openly as I fear that it is one about which many people have great reservations but on which they may be reluctant to speak frankly. It has been put to me by many people, including some Christians, that they cannot support the Bill because they cannot support the idea of state-funded Moslem schools.
>
> As a Christian I am grieved by this attitude because I believe that, as Christians, we should have enough confidence in our own faith to give our fellow citizens the democratic rights which we have given ourselves (Hansard, 4/3/91 col. 1249).

Baroness Cox then proceeded to outline three fundamental principles that she saw as underpinning the Bill. First, the principles enshrined in Article 2 of the first protocol of the European Convention on Human Rights. Second, the principle of natural justice. Third, the principles of freedom of choice, diversity of provision and encouragement of good educational standards.

The debate that followed lasted nearly four hours and covered a wide range of relevant issues. The possibility of state support for Muslim schools was certainly one of these that occupied a good deal of time. While one Lord made implicit reference to the Salman Rushdie death threat and argued that he could certainly never agree that the Islamic faith should be supported by the public purse, another gave two quotations from the Koran and claimed that they reflected the mild nature of the faith. He stated that these quotations reminded him of many Christian passages which referred to charity and love for others. Other Lords complained that the Bill could encourage public funding of schools run by religious cults such as the Moonies or Scientologists. Yet others supported the Bill because they believed that Britain should follow the lead of several of the newly formed East European countries and introduce greater diversity and choice into schooling.

The debate received considerable publicity both at the time and in the months following (O'Keeffe, 1992), for it raised many important questions about the nature of schooling and the government's understanding of parental choice of schools. However, in relation to the future activities of the Christian Schools Campaign the opening speech by the opposition, given by Baroness Blackstone, was crucial. She explained that the opposition strongly opposed the Bill on grounds of principle and because they believed that it would be unworkable in practice. But she prefaced her opposition with the following words:

> There is a good case to make all publicly maintained schools secular schools, as in the United States of America and many European countries. Religious teaching is then left to the churches and other religious bodies and takes place outside school hours rather than within them. That means that parents can be absolutely sure that the religious teaching that their children receive in the evenings or at weekends is truly in line with their own religious beliefs. It also means that children can receive their secular education together without being segregated into separate schools according to their parents' religious faith. That has much to recommend it in a multi-racial, multi-faith society. Despite the noble Baroness's disclaimers, segregation has little to recommend it. (Lords Debates, 4 March 1991, Hansard, col. 1255).

This way of thinking directly challenged much that is central to new

Christian (and Muslim) schools, for they believe that schools cannot be neutral, but that all schools automatically present their own spiritual and moral values. Indeed, as has been shown in chapter 3, it was precisely the perceived growth in secular humanist values in most state-maintained schools that drove these Christians to start their own schools.

The Christian Schools Campaign recognised that this idea of religious neutrality would have to be fought. Eventually this was done by way of the 1992 Education (Schools) Act.

6 Religious neutrality and the 1992 Education (Schools) Act

The myth of religious neutrality

The 1991 debate in the House of Lords received considerable media coverage, and it was inevitable that the British situation would be compared with that of other countries. While supporters of diversity and state funding of a variety of religiously-based schools looked to Denmark and The Netherlands for inspiration (Walford, 1995b), opponents argued that Britain would be better served by following countries such as the United States of America, where religion and education are Constitutionally separated. As indicated in the previous chapter, Baroness Blackstone had started her opposition to Baroness Cox's Bill with the words:

> There is a good case to make all publicly maintained schools secular schools, as in the United States of America and many European countries. Religious teaching is then left to the churches and other religious bodies and takes place outside school hours rather than within them. That means that parents can be absolutely sure that the religious teaching that their children receive in the evenings or at weekends is truly in line with their own religious beliefs. It also means that children can receive their secular education together without being segregated into separate schools according to their parents' religious faith. That has much to recommend it in a multi-racial, multi-faith society. Despite the Baroness's disclaimers, segregation has little to recommend it. (Lords Debates, 4 March 1991, Hansard, col. 1255).

The idea that it is possible for schools can be free of religious belief directly challenges much that is central to the new Christian schools (and the Muslim schools), for they believe that schools cannot be neutral, but that they present their own spiritual and moral values. The Christian Schools Campaign recognised that what they saw as 'the myth of religious neutrality' (Clouser, 1991) would have to be fought as part of the wider campaign for state funding.

By the time the debate in March 1991, the main purpose of proceeding with Baroness Cox's Bill was to raise discussion about faith-based schools and to maintain momentum in the Campaign. In practice, it not only achieved considerable media coverage, but also enabled the Campaign to identify members of the Lords and Commons who were supportive. Various proposals were made about how to proceed. One idea (which the Director of the Campaign, Ruth Deakin, claimed was suggested by Brian Griffiths) was to establish a Commission of Enquiry into faith-based schooling. Ideally, this would be a Royal Commission, but it was immediately evident that a semi-independent commission would be all that was possible. To give greater visibility to the Commission the Director of the Campaign, in consultation with Baroness Cox, tried to persuade a Peer to Chair the Commission. Lord Pearson, who had been active in the debate, declined the offer, but Lord Northbourne, who had not taken part in the debate but had expressed support to Baroness Cox, agreed to act as Chair. His view was that an eminent academic should be found to oversee the research side of the Commission.

Professor Keith Watson of the University of Reading was chosen to manage the research side of the proposed Commission. He is an active evangelical Christian himself, and was at that point supervising a graduate student's doctoral research about the new Christian schools. However, when Ruth Deakin, Professor Watson and Lord Northbourne met together to discuss the details of the remit for the Commission, they came to the conclusion that it might be more profitable to switch track and tackle what they saw as the main problem raised in the 1991 debate - the 'myth of religious neutrality' - in another way. The 1991 Education (Schools) Bill on school inspection was currently before Parliament, so it was decided that, rather than again tackle the funding issue head on, it would be better to bring forward amendments to that Bill that would challenge the 'myth of neutrality' (Deakin and Jones, 1993). The proposal for a Commission was shelved and Lord Northbourne agreed to table and support suitable amendments to the 1991 Education (Schools) Bill.

The 1992 Education (Schools) Act

The main purposes of the 1992 Education (Schools) Act were to establish new Her Majesty's Inspectorates for England and Wales, to provide the necessary legislation for regular inspections of schools by new privatized teams of inspectors and to give the Secretaries of State more powers to require schools to publish information. It was, of course, a very controversial Bill and many amendments were tabled in both the Lords and Commons.

The small, but highly significant, group of amendments tabled by Lord Northbourne had three objectives. The first part was to require all schools to:

> publish, in such manner as may be prescribed, information on the spiritual, moral and cultural values upon which education is provided in the school and the manner in which the spiritual, moral and cultural development of pupils is achieved.

This, it was argued, would ensure that parents were able to take this information into consideration when making their choice of school. In a similar way, the second part would require the new inspection teams to report on the 'spiritual, moral and cultural values' of each school, and the third part would require the Chief Inspector to inform the Secretary of State for Education about the spiritual, moral and cultural values of all schools.

One interesting aspect about the wording of these amendments was that they echoed parts of previous Education Acts. Thus the 1944 Education Act (chapter 31, Section 7) states that:

> The statutory system of public education shall be organised in three progressive stages to be known as primary education, secondary education, and further education; and it shall be the duty of the local education authority for every area, so far as their powers extend, to contribute towards the spiritual, moral, mental, and physical development of the community by securing that efficient education throughout those stages shall be available to meet the needs of the population of their area.

These ideas are repeated in the 1988 Education Reform Act (Chapter 40, section 1, (2)) where it is stated that the curriculum shall promote 'the spiritual, moral, cultural, mental and physical development of pupils at the school and of society'.

This choice of wording was carefully thought through, and the final drafting of the amendments was made by activists in the Christian Schools Campaign in cooperation with the far larger campaigning organization - Christians in Education.

The involvement of Christians in Education (CiE) was significant for, somewhat paradoxically, the Christian Schools Campaign had practically ceased to exist as a separate organization by the middle of 1992. Although the Campaign had sprung from the Christian Schools Trust, there had been constant tensions within the group of schools about the campaign. As will be shown later, some new Christian schools were actually firmly against the idea of funding from the state - especially if it meant that Muslim schools would also be funded. Others saw problems of compromise with the political Right, and feared that they had become involved with policies very much against their own beliefs. The result was that those active in the CSC simply transferred their allegiances to another organization with which they already had contacts. This was Christians in Education, which by that time had become a Department of CARE (Christian Action Research and Education), which itself had developed from the Nationwide Festival of Light of the 1970s.

CARE has considerable experience of lobbying Parliament on a range of issues. It runs a substantial office near to Westminster and produces high quality documentation for its supporters. It has been concerned with such issues as Sunday Trading, euthanasia, pornography, abortion, divorce, and child abuse. Education has been a major focus, particularly religious education and faith-based schools. The organization has developed considerable sophistication in its methods. Apart from regular newsletters and prayer diaries to supporters, it also produces *Care Parliamentary Update for Activists* five times each year which gives detailed information on current campaigns. Following an outline report on the state and results of each campaign is a list of 'action points' which usually include how to obtain further information, and encouragement to visit or write to MPs, EMPs, or other significant people. CARE produces its own information videos and books related to its campaigns and distributes material produced by others where it is relevant. In 1993 it produced its own handbook on the need for Christians to become involved in public debate and political action and on how to do so (Whitcomb and Williams, 1993).

CARE and CiE had developed and interest in new Christian schools during the late 1980s but, by 1992, CiE had taken up the battle for state funding of Christian schools. It was a combined CiE/CSC group that drafted the amendments and initiated the crucial interventions in the 1992 Act.

The Education (Schools) Bill had its formal First Reading in the House of Lords on 31 January 1992, and Second Reading on 11 February. Lord Northbourne used the Second Reading debate in a traditional way to indicate that he intended to bring forward amendments at the Committee Stage. The speech was relatively short, but included a discussion of the difficulty of defining the word 'values' and gave examples that considered both discipline and religious teaching. Baroness Blatch, who, as Minister of State, was guiding the Bill through the Lords, stated that she was sympathetic to the aims of Lord Northbourne's amendments but argued that they were unnecessary, as previous legislation and the 1992 Bill already covered what was stipulated in the amendments.

In his speech at the Committee Stage on 24 February, Lord Northbourne tackled Baroness Blatch's stated reasons for not accepting the amendments. He argued that existing legislation could be interpreted as covering the content of his amendments only by making special assumptions about the words 'education' and 'curriculum' within the Bill. He argued that 'there is a need for a clause in the Bill which clearly and unequivocally directs inspectors to report on the whole school, including the ethos and values in and out of the classroom' (Lords Debates, 24 February, 1992, Hansard, col. 97). Lord Northbourne expressed the need for such a report in the following terms:

> The Government have opted for diversity. Without doubt, sooner or later, some ideological groups - they may be political, religious or something else - will gain sufficient control of some of our schools to influence the values which are transmitted to the pupils. Some of those values many not be what some parents want for their children. Some could be inimical to a pluralistic and liberal democracy; for example, values in relation to equal opportunities, to the role of women and girls in society and to racial issues. Inspectors visiting such schools could be under considerable pressure not to report on such issues unless they are clearly and unambiguously required to do so by law (Lords Debates, 24 February, 1992, Hansard, col. 98).

If parents were to have the right to choose their child's school, Lord Northbourne argued, they need as full a picture as possible. This included data on 'its ethos and values as well as its academic success'. Information provided through school prospectuses and inspectors' reports should reflect this need.

Lord Northbourne was then supported in speeches by Baroness Strange, the Lord Bishop of Guildford, Lord Rochester, Lord Pearson of Rannoch, Baroness Warnock, Lord Elton, Baroness Faithfull, and Lord Peston. Baroness Strange, for example, expressed her support as:

> ...a school is there to teach and impart knowledge. For that, parents must see that the school follows the national curriculum. That is the level of the mind. Human beings also have another dimension: they have the dimension of the spirit. Parents may be Christian, Jewish, Moslems or have no faith at all. However, they wish their children to be educated in the same way. Whatever their views, it is the right of parents to know what are the spiritual, moral and cultural values of the school so that they can choose a school which approximates best to what they wish for their own children (Lord Debates, 24 February 1992, Hansard, col. 99).

Lord Elton was equally forthright:

> Any prospectus of a school which is silent on matters of its moral and spiritual standards is deficient in a crucial and important area... Educationists refer to something called 'affective curriculum'. The affective curriculum, in layman's language, means things that are taught by mistake or unconsciously. A great deal is taught in schools by mistake or unconsciously and is much more readily perceived by people on the outside than by those who have been inside the school for a long time.

In the whole debate there were no speeches against the amendments and only three speakers expressed hesitations. Baroness Warnock, for example, supported explicit directions to inspectors, but believed that what was to be published in prospectuses was a matter of no importance as it would result in platitudes. Lord Beloff said that he wished he could support the amendments but believed that it was impossible to select inspectors with the necessary cultural or ethical characteristics through a process of competitive tendering. Baroness Seear felt that 'nobody is going to disagree with the idea that in theory one should support [the amendments]', but argued that objective inspection of values was very difficult.

This degree of support had not been anticipated when the amendments were first drafted. In an interview about a month before the debate, Ruth Deakin stated that Lord Northbourne believed that 'it definitely would not get through as an amendment, but it would cause a debate, which would probably cause a furore'. In spite of the ability of CARE to mount a large campaign, this had not, in fact, occurred. Very little lobbying of Peers had been done by Christians in Education or anyone else, with the exception of a simple letter to about 150 peers sent by the Campaigns Director of CARE. This letter was sent on 18 February 1992 to draw Peers' attention to the amendments and ask for their support. It included a briefing note that explained the background to the amendments and their wording, and argued that the greater diversity of schools made it increasingly important that parents were aware of the spiritual, moral and cultural values of schools.

There was only a very low level campaign to support the amendments, yet Peers were clear that they opposed the Government and wished to have the amendments accepted into the Bill. While sponsors of the amendments merely expected them to raise once again the debate about 'value neutrality' within schools, the impossibility of such a concept was already accepted by all speakers. The debate made clear that speakers fully accepted that schools reflected and expressed values in all that they did and, indeed, this was seen as an essential part of schooling.

After about three-quarters of an hour of one-sided support for the amendments, Baroness Blatch replied. In a considered speech, regarding inspection, she stated, 'I have been impressed with the points made by the noble Lords from all sides of the Committee...I should like to think more about the matter and about these amendments before Report stage and possibly to consider bringing back amendments in a similar vein' (Lords Debates, 24 February, 1992, Hansard, col. 107). She also went on to say that, in response to points made by Lord Elton (who had chaired the Enquiry into Discipline in Schools), she would also consider whether this section should be extended to include the social development of pupils such that behavioural and other aspects could be fully covered in the inspectors' reports. However, on the question of what should be published by schools Baroness Blatch said that she still felt that this was better dealt with through Regulation, and that no new legislation was required. In response to this statement, Lord Northbourne withdrew his amendments.

Further debate on 2 March 1992 made it clear that the Government was prepared to put forward their own amendments such that all aspects of school life were to be inspected - not just the subjects taught during lesson time - and were to be included in the reports, and that Lord Northbourne's amendments were to be modified to include the word 'social' as well as 'spiritual, moral and cultural'. These changes were made, and the 1992 Education (Schools) Act subsequently stated that:

> It shall be the general duty of any registered inspector conducting an inspection under this section to report on -
> (a) the quality of education provided by the school;
> (b) the educational standards achieved by the school;
> (c) whether the financial resources made available to the school are managed efficiently; and
> (d) the spiritual, moral, social and cultural development of pupils at the school.' (Section 9, 4.)

In a similar way, duties were placed upon the Chief Inspectors of England and of Wales to inform their respective Secretaries of State about these four aspects.

> In her summing-up speech Baroness Blatch stated:
> The noble Lord, Lord Northbourne, has been instrumental in persuading the House - although I have to say that the House succumbed readily to the case he made - that the spiritual, moral, cultural and social dimensions of education should be made subject to inspectorial scrutiny. I was impressed with his case from the start and I am delighted that the appropriate form of words was agreed and now form part of the Bill. (Lords Debates, 12 March, 1992, Hansard, col. 1450.)

Interpretation

This particular part of the campaign was unusual. It is clearly not a case where a pressure group has acted to persuade others to its point of view by the weight of its argument or by rational discussion. To recapitulate: the main purpose of the 1992 Education (Schools) Bill was to move schooling further into the marketplace by giving parents greater information on schools and by privatizing the inspectorate. Parents were to be encouraged to select schools for their children within a competitive market of schools on the basis of examination results and inspectors' reports. It was a deeply ideological Bill, and there were many of all political persuasions who doubted the wisdom of further increasing the competition between schools and of establishing a fully privatized schools' inspectorate where schools were able to choose their own inspection team on the basis of competitive tenders. It was also a Bill that was tightly timetabled, for a General Election was due before June 1992. Its date (9 April) was announced before the Bill finally became law. If the Bill was to become law, it was necessary for the Government to be prepared to acknowledge and respond to some the criticisms made of it. Thus, although the Government had clear majorities in both the House of Commons and the House of Lords, it was defeated on several important features of the legislation. The two most important changes were that the Government was forced to concede that Ofsted (rather than the schools themselves) should select the inspection teams, and that LEAs should retain the right to inspect schools in their areas where circumstances required it.

In many ways the acceptance of the Northbourne amendments might be seen as just another case of the Government's conceding to pressure to ensure that the Bill became law. After all, it did not challenge the basic ideology of the Bill, it merely added another dimension to the factors on which parents should be able to choose. However, the undercurrent behind many of the speeches in the House of Lords was that the speakers wished to widen the Government's narrow vision of the purposes of schooling beyond that of examination successes. The Government's original proposals were highly influenced by the New Right in education, with the neo-conservative element championing the importance of 'league tables' of examination results while the neo-liberal wing emphasising the need for 'freedom of the market' in inspection. Although, 'league tables' or even 'examination results' are not mentioned in the Act, various speeches from the Government made it clear that the legislation requiring information from all schools (including independent schools) was designed to ensure that such 'league tables' could be constructed. Parents were expected to use this information to help them in choosing schools for their children and the information was intended to increase public awareness of the quality of education provided by the schools concerned.

Most of those in the House of Lords, many of whom have extensive backgrounds in education, were less committed than the Government to pure ideological posturings and had a wider and more complex view of the nature and purposes of education. They wished to indicate that examination results were only a part the concerns of education and Lord Northbourne's amendments enabled them to emphasise further factors. The previous debate in 1991 about the desirability or possibility of 'value neutral' schools was forgotten in the rush to insist that the concerns of schools went beyond examinations, and the possibility of a value-neutral school was simply legislated out of existence.

What is interesting about the acceptance of the amendments is that there appears to have been very little micro-political activity from the proposers or anyone else. As they expected the amendments simply to generate debate and be rejected, the proposers initiated only minimal micro-political activity (Ball, 1987, 1990). The circular letter was sent to about 150 Peers and a few were contacted informally, but there was little of the tactical manoeuvrings, use of power, building of support, and so on that we associate with micro-politics. There is little evidence for any substantial behind-the-scenes negotiation or any process of compromise and trade-off.

At this micro-level, the acceptance of Lord Northbourne's amendments may be far more easily understood in terms of Cohen et al's (1972) 'garbage can' model of organizational choice. This model emphasises the instability and unpredictability of institutional life, and proposes that ambiguity is a common feature of many organizations. Such organizations tend to share three characteristics: problematic goals, unclear technology and fluid participation (Bush, 1994). An organization may be said to have problematic goals if it operates on a variety of inconsistent and ill-defined preferences. It can be said to have unclear technology if it has lack of understanding of its own processes and operates on the basis of accidents of past experiences. And it has fluid participation if participants in the organization vary among themselves the time and effort they devote to the organization, and where individual participants vary from one time to another. Such characteristics are evident in 'organized anarchies', and they may exhibit 'garbage can' decision-making.

Choice opportunities (garbage cans) are situations or occasions where the organization is expected to produce behaviour that subsequently may be called a decision. There is a discontinuous flow of problems, solutions, participants and choice opportunities without there necessarily being any 'logical' or one-to-one relationship between these four elements. Thus solutions are seen as products looking for a choice opportunity and a group of problems to which to fit. In highly politicised settings, opportunities are seized as they present themselves and as events unfold.

As Enderud (1977: 53) clarifies:

The name of the model, the 'garbage can' model, originates from the metaphor of viewing choice opportunities as open cans into which

86

participants can 'dump' problems or solutions. By using a certain amount of energy (a function of the number and mix of problems and solutions) the can is removed from the scene and the choice is made.

The model has been successfully applied to a growing number of organizations. It has been shown, for example, that decision-making within educational establishments can often be illuminated through this perspective. For example, the originators of the idea, Cohen and March (1974), applied their model of organized anarchies to American universities, while Bell (1989), examined the turbulent environment that existed within a school that had been formed by amalgamation of three preexisting secondary schools.

The case of the Northbourne amendments shows that the House of Lords may also sometimes act as an organized anarchy, and that, in such circumstances, the 'garbage can' model has some explanatory utility. In this case the participants were those Peers present, the group of problems centred on the desire to attack the narrowness of the Government's emphasis on examination results, and the choice opportunity was provided by the debate. Lord Northbourne's amendments provided an acceptable 'solution' to the set of problems, and they were seized opportunistically. There may well have been other 'solutions' that would have 'solved' their problems, but this one surfaced at the appropriate time and it sufficed.

It is important to note, however, that this particular 'solution' was acceptable because it allowed Peers to show their displeasure without attacking the fundamentals of the Government's position. It simply broadened the criteria on which parents were expected to base their choice of school. The wider macro-structures of power help define which of the 'solutions' in the garbage can were actually acceptable in this situation: Conservative Lords were only prepared to push so far in the direction they wished to go. Correspondingly, the Government was only willing to accept those parts of the amendments that would not seriously infringe their future flexibility: they did not wish to have what was to be published in primary legislation, but stated that the details would be put in Regulations. Thus, even though the 'garbage can' model is based on a degree of irrationality and opportunism, the examination of particular cases where it can be applied still gives insights into the complexities of power at the macro-level.

The result was an unexpected and highly significant change in the law. A small group of activists had managed to insist that the new inspectorate would examine and report on the spiritual and moral values projected by each school.

As will be discussed in chapter eight, the nature of what was to be inspected and the details of how this was to be done remained to be fought over, but the change marked a solid victory for the Christian Schools Campaign in association with Christians in Education.

7 The demise of the Christian Schools Campaign

It was stated in the last chapter that, by the time the Northbourne amendments were debated, the Christian Schools Campaign was working closely with Christians in Education (CiE) and Christian Action, Research and Education (CARE). In practice, the Christian Schools Campaign drifted to closure over a long period. The Director, Ruth Deakin, resigned in July 1992. There followed a long period of little activity and the CSC was officially wound-up about a year later.

The closure of CSC as a separate campaigning organization was the culmination of many long-term tensions within the Campaign and differences between those involved with the Christian Schools Trust and the Christian Schools Campaign. The divisions were also indicative of some deep differences of opinion and belief within the wider Christian schools movement. However, before exploring these internal divisions in detail, it is worth considering the changing position of one of the most well-known Patrons of the campaign.

The Archbishop as Patron

The Rt Rev Dr George Carey became a Patron of the Christian Schools Campaign in 1990 while he was Bishop of Bath and Wells. This was a logical move as the Campaign was launched within his Diocese and had its office at Oak Hill School in Bristol. Furthermore his Chaplain, Rev Richard Russell, was also a Patron. Dr Carey was enthroned as Archbishop of Canterbury on 19 April 1991, coincidentally one the same day as a National Christian Education Conference in

Nottingham organized by the Christian Schools Trust. Understandably, those involved with the Christian Schools Campaign were delighted that Dr Carey had been selected and, at that conference, were able to celebrate his enthronement. By September they had different feelings.

On 19 September 1991 the new Archbishop gave his first speech to the Anglican Secondary School Heads at Chester. In that speech, he argued for the importance of church schools and the continued involvement of the Church of England in education. He gave a historical overview of the Church's role in education which included the work of the National Society in the early nineteenth century and the Sunday School movement in the late eighteenth, arguing that 'the primary aim was to improve the possibility that ordinary young people might aspire to a life which was more satisfying - morally, spiritually and physically'. It was a well argued, and largely uncontentious, case.

About half way through the speech, however, Carey moved on to make comments that seemed designed with sensationalist journalists in mind. He said:

> The point about Christian education is that it offers a holistic framework which takes people through life and prepares them for destiny with God. But we are often told that such talk in a secularised world is unfashionable and out of date. We are told that this is a 'climate of unbelief' and that materialism rules. And it is that kind of talk which is driving Christians to set up protected schools in which the Christian faith can be taught in an atmosphere of tolerance and love. It is the same driving instinct which is behind other faith communities wanting to start their own schools in which the religious values they believe in may be protected from the harsh and cold winds of an indifferent and secular world. However, I do not believe that we should concede the case so readily. The vast majority of the people in this land are not unbelievers who, having considered the case for God, have turned away from him in favour of a godless, cruel and indifferent universe where no absolute and eternal values reign. On the contrary most of our fellow citizens do believe in God, do pray and do believe that Christian morality is important - however tenuous their links may be with the local church...

> ... the kind of education I am interested in is not only the rediscovery and repossession of a Christian world view but the breadth of vision in which the individual's growth is physical, intellectual, moral and spiritual. And we

are not talking about brain washing or indoctrination, but in an open system in which doubt, questioning, argument and enquiry are allowable and essential ingredients. That is why, in my opinion, the desire on the part of some Christians to send their children to tightly protected Christian schools, in which no alternatives to the Christian faith are known, is socially divisive, educationally damaging and spiritually unsatisfying - because the time will come when unpalatable realities will have to be faced - and often it is done when there is no structure of support to see the student through the threat of collapse. I remain convinced that the Anglican pattern of open education, rooted in a firm Christian base and a loving Christian environment is a better context for growth.
(Transcript of speech given by George Carey, 19/9/91.)

He did not mention the Christian Schools Campaign, or any new Christian Schools by name, but the *Times Educational Supplement* claimed that 'Dr Carey turns on his own campaign' (Lodge, 1991b). According to the article, Carey had delivered a strong attack on the Christian Schools Campaign, and this was certainly a reasonable interpretation. Although the attack was heavily coded, it was an astonishing speech, that was given without any prior consultation with the Christian Schools Campaign. As far as those involved in the Campaign knew, Dr Carey still supported the aims of the Campaign. His name was listed on the Campaign's notepaper, on Press Releases and other documents, and he had not previously raised any questions or doubts about the nature of the schools or the Campaign.

A little later, members of the Campaign met with Dr Carey. Apparently his official position now meant that he was unable to support a group that appeared to be in some opposition to Church of England schools. He offered his resignation, and it was accepted.

It was a strange incident, but it indicated some of the tensions between Christians about the desirability and nature of separate Christian schools. While some schools linked to the Christian Schools Trust were certainly designed to be separatist and did teach a narrow view of Christianity, others were far broader in their views and encouraged discussion and debate about belief in the way the Archbishop suggested was necessary. But the Church of England's view of its role in education meant that it was unable to officially support and schools that might be considered as separatist, and it was thus unable to support the Campaign. The differences between the new Christian schools meant that only some were actually problematic, but they all had to be officially rejected.

Divisions within the Campaign

As discussed in chapter two and by Poyntz and Walford (1994) a survey of the schools with links to the Christian Schools Trust was conducted in the early months of 1993. Besides the information already discussed, the survey asked specifically for views about the Campaign and about whether the responding school was likely to apply for state funding. One most surprising finding was that, while there were 65 schools associated with the Christian Schools Trust, and the Christian Schools Campaign sprang from the Trust, far from all of the schools were in agreement with the aims of the Campaign (Walford, 1994c). In answer to a specific question about whether the school agreed with the aims of the Christian Schools Campaign, 55 per cent did agree, 14 per cent clearly stated that they did not agree, and a further 30 per cent were unsure or did not know. Further, it was clear from the replies that several schools did not distinguish between the Trust and the Campaign, and that some had little idea of what the Campaign was about. In addition, a few of the schools pointed out that they were unable to answer the questions on the Campaign as its future was at that point under discussion. In total, only 19 per cent of the schools said that they supported the Campaign financially, while 42 per cent said that they supported the Campaign in prayer.

This is a surprisingly low level of support for a Campaign that was being conducted in the name of the schools involved. Even more startling was the degree of antipathy, for 19 per cent of the schools said that they would never accept government funding. Some heads in interview and on the questionnaires showed a fierce opposition to the idea of government funding on the basis that they believed that God would provide for His own work and that no government should be allowed to interfere in the running of their schools.
For example, one respondent wrote:

> My stand point [is] clear as one who would not tolerate government interference on the issue of education. I believe most Christian schools are set up to be independent and thus able to follow what they believe is the best route to follow. Any compromise on this idealism (i.e. teaching evolution as fact, deviant sex education, acceptance of other faiths as

alternatives etc) would soon weaken their stand and nullify their reason for existence. Any move by government to enforce the national curriculum would have to be resisted, preferably in a united manner, and (though I have no love of law courts and their expense) through the law courts. Any acceptance of Government funds is an immediate weakening of the independent status of schools, and is not acceptable in *any* circumstances. [Q.54.]

One head of a larger school was equally adamant in interview:

I am absolutely against state funding. The Campaign is trying to have it both ways by being independent and also accepting funding from the state. Christian schools should be dependent upon God, not the government. The only way I would accept money from the government was if it was offered with absolutely no stipulations. [I.6.]

Another headteacher of a large well-established school claimed:

Well, the reason we don't want funding - we wouldn't accept it even if the government offered it to us, because when we first came here, when God first began to speak to us, He very clearly showed us that we were not to have fees or salaries. He really laid down so clearly the future of the school, which has come to pass, that we knew we were not to have any help at all - that He would supply our needs. You see, if we came under the government..., for example, they're not allowed any physical punishment in schools. A minor thing in a way, but it's not the way we want to run the school. And although we hardly ever do [use it], we don't want to be tied down to things we feel would not be right for us, so we want to keep clear of involvement with those who don't believe. [I.1.]

Even where schools supported the Campaign both financially and in prayer, this did not necessarily mean that they wished to obtain grant-maintained status for themselves. It was frequently argued that the Campaign was about 'righteousness' as much as money, and that it was a matter of 'justice' that parents should not have to 'pay twice' for their children's education - once through their taxes and again at a private Christian school because they were dissatisfied with state schools. This support for the 'righteousness' of the Campaign meant that the particular 'solution' of grant-maintained status that was on offer did not satisfy all schools.

Objections and difficulties to the possibility of grant-maintained status centred on a number of areas. The right to give corporal punishment (which is still allowed in private schools) was one common issue. Of the 48 schools answering the question, 83 per cent used corporal punishment. It was often made clear that corporal punishment was only used as a last resort and several said that it had not been actually used in the last few years, but the threat was maintained. For some schools, the prohibition on the use of corporal punishment was sufficient for them to not apply for state funding, for they believed that it was a Biblical injunction. Others recognised that they might well be able to avoid this prohibition by asking parents to administer corporal punishment on behalf of the school. Others schools did not see corporal punishment as a central issue, but on the results of a simple tick-box question, fifty-three per cent stated that they would not accept government funding if this meant that corporal punishment was prohibited.

On the same simple tick-box list, 36 per cent of the schools stated that they would not accept government funding if they had to teach the National Curriculum. Certain aspects of what these headteachers perceived the National Curriculum to require were thought to be in opposition to the mission of these schools. For example, 42 per cent of the schools did not teach sex education, and a few of these were strongly against this happening in schools. Their belief was that it was the parents' responsibility to teach sex education. In particular, although specific questions on AIDS teaching were not asked, it became evident in some interviews that some heads were very strongly opposed to teaching about AIDS as they considered it might encourage 'deviant sexuality'.

Other clear areas of difficulty to most schools were those directly associated with Christian faith. All but one of the schools taught creation as fact, and most treated evolution as an incorrect theory. However, some 30 per cent did not teach evolution at all. Multi-faith teaching and worship in state-maintained schools was often one of the major reasons for establishing these Christian schools, so the issue of the teaching of other faiths was of obvious importance. While many of the schools did teach about other faiths, this appeared to be usually in the context of those other faiths being incorrect. Some schools were fiercely opposed to teaching about other faiths. One very outspoken head expressed this as:

Well, we wouldn't [teach multi-faith]. That's why we wouldn't want funding. I don't want a politician telling me what to teach and what not to teach, since most politicians are only in politics because they have no intelligence to do anything else. [I.11.]

Other factors that would dissuade schools from accepting government money related to the student and staff intakes. Thirty-two per cent of the schools stated they would not accept funding if this meant they had to take more (or any) non-Christian children. Many of the schools already took a proportion of non-Christian children, including Sikhs and Muslims, but wanted to restrict the numbers. A very few had a majority of non-Christian children. Others took only Christians, and wished to retain that right. Controls over staffing were of major significance for all of the schools. Christian teachers were seen as crucial to what a Christian school was, and all but one of the schools would not accept government money if it meant they had to accept any (more) non-Christian teachers.

Finally, several of the schools were philosophically and religiously opposed to the whole idea of receiving state funding. They believed that the bible instructed parents to educate their children and that this responsibility should not be given to the state. One headteacher explained:

The other thing is that we would have to think very carefully about whether we wanted to be a state school. Because, philosophically, I don't believe in state education. I don't think it's right, because it's not biblical. In the bible the state has the right to levy taxes, to provide law and order and punishment for those who don't keep within the law, but nowhere has it any authority to provide education for children. Whereas parents are responsible for the education of their children, and the church has some responsibility as well. And I think that the state has highjacked education... So we would have strong reservations about opting-in to a state education system that we basically don't believe in...We have found that God has supplied all our needs financially so we are not rushing down the road for state money. [I.2.]

A similar viewpoint was set out in a leaflet published in 1991 (Baxter, 1991) which attacked the Campaign and the arguments put forward in support of the Campaign in a booklet by the Director (Deakin, 1989a). Although Baxter was not associated with the Christian Schools Trust, his arguments are similar to those used by Christians within the group. His case centred on the role of the state in education:

> Let us pose a question. Who owns our children? Is it the State or parents? Both answers have been given in the past and are given today. Actually, neither is correct. According to the Bible God owns everything since he created everything. Therefore God owns our children, not the State *nor* parents. God, however, delegates to parents the responsibility of nurturing and training the children he gives them. Parents are stewards of a God given gift. This responsibility is never given to the State in the Bible. The State is never given the role of being a substitute parent.

> What then is the role of the State? As spelled out in Romans 13 the State's role is to protect and encourage those who do good and punish evil doers. Nowhere in the Bible is the State given a role as a welfare agent. In the Bible the family is the unit of welfare. Taxation in the Bible never went to the poor and the needy, nor education. The State's role was never to *enable* parents to fulfill their God given responsibilities by providing funding for education raised by means of taxation (Baxter, 1991: 2).

Baxter's view is that, rather than Christians seeking state support for their own schools, a long term aim should be to work towards the complete abolition and cessation of all tax financed education. He claims that education is 'a commodity like anything else' and that parents should not expect their children to 'get educated at someone else's expense' (p.3). While this pamphlet expressed its viewpoint in stark and somewhat simplistic form, the general position was one that was accepted by many of those in the Christian Schools Trust grouping. Several of the schools in the group made it clear that their constitution or Trust Deeds had been drawn-up specifically to prohibit the schools from obtaining funding from the state.

Some heads saw the Campaign itself as being misguided, especially as it might lead to other faiths being able to obtain government money for their own schools. Talking of the Campaign, one head of a large school with a strong traditional academic emphasis stated:

> I fear that they will have set in course something that I will loath. Firstly, Muslims will then have the right to their schools, and the whole sectarian

filth will come into this place. And J.W.s [Jehovah's Witnesses] will have a right to set up schools, Mormons will have a right to set up schools - and I'm totally against it.

This same head was equally scathing about some of the schools linked to the Trust:

> Now a lot of these house groups are freakish, and I'm against them, because I see the freakishness and the control that the leaders are exerting over people. Now a lot of these groups have discipleship, heavy shepherding, and while they may have come out of that movement, while they have changed their face, they are just the same, and the men who control it are tyrannical. And I find a horror in thinking that [the Campaign] unwittingly is helping to gain government money for such movements. And I think there are a lot of well-meaning Christians who will get on the bandwagon if they think they can get state money, and it will really be to help subsidize their churches not for the good of the children. And that is my worry, for in the end what we care about is children, and I feel for the kids who will unwittingly get involved in it because their parents are desperate to escape from the morass of state education. [I.11.]

Additional tensions within the campaign

The divisions over the Campaign were indications of other tensions between the schools associated with the Christian Schools Trust. The most fundamental of these tensions was theological and related to basic differences in their views of how Christians come to know God's will and the role of the Bible in directing everyday lives. All would believe that the Bible was Divinely inspired, but there were differences in interpreting exactly what this meant. While some believed that the Bible was a sufficient guide to all aspects of life, and that it showed Christians what to do in all circumstances, others admitted that the Bible was not always clear, and that individual Christians had to make decisions for themselves in the light of the more general message of the Bible. Again, while some believed that God intervenes in the everyday lives of Christians to cause them to meet certain people or to have particular conversations, others believed that Christians will have times when they did not know what God wants them to do, and that they must make the best decisions they can.

While the first group were likely to interpret the meaning of the Bible as literally as possible and generally regarded the message as being unchangeable for all times, those Christians in the second group were more prepared to interpret the message of the Bible in the light of changing social and political contexts. Thus they might argue that, while particular regulations and prohibitions were appropriate for first century Palestine under Roman occupation, they did not necessarily have universal applicability.

A good example of differences in interpretation concerned the role of women in the Church. The leadership of the Christian Schools Trust was male dominated and none of the Churches with which schools had links would have countenanced the idea of a female minister. Thus, some of those involved with the Christian Schools Trust found difficulty in accepting that the Director of the Christian Schools Campaign was a woman. Even among those who accepted this role for a woman, some would carefully define the 'leadership role' that she had. For example, one head who was a member of the Steering Group stated:

> The Steering Group of the Campaign have always believed that Ruth was God's woman for this particular time. It was she who was blessed with the contacts and the conversations. God's hand was clearly on her to talk to the right people at the right time. None of us could claim that degree of anointing - so here was God's woman, for now, to do a particular task.

But, while the Director was a woman, the Steering Group for the Campaign was always male dominated, and where women were appointed to the Steering Group they tended to leave rather quickly. As the same member of the Steering Group stated:

> I think [women in positions of leadership] has been a particular problem for certain streams in the Church. We would still believe in the headship of the man, but that is not to mean the woman inferior, or to suggest that it is only the man who has the gifts and the right, responsibility to work out those gifts.

The final demise of the Christian Schools Campaign was messy. There were disagreements about the future direction of the Trust and the Campaign. At one point there were thoughts that it would be sensible for the Christian Schools

Trust to formally merge with Christians in Education and to cease being a separate organization. This merger with the more powerful CiE and CARE would have increased the resources of both. If the Trust were to join with CiE, then the Campaign would follow. The Trust made unsuccessful initial contacts with CiE, but personal links between those involved with the Campaign and some of the activists in CiE proved more profitable. Some of those who were Trustees and on the Council of Reference of the Trust then changed their minds about possible merger with CiE. Separate letters were sent from the Trust and from the Campaign to all the headteachers involved with CST. There was no open vote, but the Trustees decided to remain a separate organization. The Director of CSC, Ruth Deakin, resigned in July 1992.

The confusion about the closure of the Campaign is illustrated through the various issues of the *Christian Schools Newsletter*. From December 1989 to March 1992 eight issues were published. These short magazines of 8 or 12 pages were mainly concerned with news of the schools, testimonies, comment and ideas for teaching, but seven out of eight of these first issues carried a substantial section giving news of the campaign. Moreover, from issue three onwards, the full list of Patrons and members of the Steering Committee of the Christian Schools Campaign was given on the back page, in equal prominence to the list of Trustees and Council of Reference of the Christian Schools Trust. Issue 9 of June 1992 was a simple two page sheet, and from issue 10 onwards (March 1993) there was no mention of the Christian Schools Campaign at all. No explanation of the change was given in any of the Newsletters. In the July 1993 issue the name of the Newsletter was changed to the *Christian Schools Trust Newsletter* which made the shift in emphasis clear. That issue also published a letter from the Director of CiE, Anne Holt, which spoke of the developing relationship between CiE and the CST. She said:

Christians in Education (CiE) continues to encourage and be encouraged by the 'new independent' Christian schools in this country. We consider you to be an important element in God's scheme of things, in the maintenance of his witness to Christ, not only as individuals but through corporate structures... Many of you will know already that CiE has actively lobbied government to legislate so that faith-based schools could receive funding if they want to. It looks as though this possibility is coming closer. Not every school will want to go that way but we hope that some will sense the Lord's leading in this direction, to be yet another kind of Christian model (Holt, 1993).

The Christian Schools Campaign was dead, but it was never allowed a decent funeral. It seems that it was inappropriate to talk about the dead.

8 Inspecting values and the 1993 Education Act

Inspecting values

The 1992 Education (Schools) Act passed into law in 16 March, and a General Election was called for 9 April. Following yet another Conservative victory, Kenneth Clarke was replaced by John Patten, an active Roman Catholic. The appointment of an active Christian to the post of Secretary of State for Education probably had significant repercussions, both in the way the 1992 Act was implemented and in the content of the White Paper *Choice and Diversity* (DFE, 1992).

Those involved with the Northbourne amendments to the 1992 Act were well aware that legislation is only the first step towards successful implementation. The Act imposed a general duty on the Chief Inspectors for England and Wales to keep the Secretaries of State informed about the 'spiritual, moral, social and cultural development of pupils at schools', and gave the specific duty to registered inspectors to include in their inspection a report on 'the spiritual, moral, social and cultural development of pupils at that school'. However, the way in which these duties were enacted would depend on the interpretations given to them by those with power in the new Office for Standards in Education (Ofsted) and the Department for Education. The need for further political pressure was recognised (Deakin and Jones, 1993).

Of central importance was the degree to which 'spiritual and moral' were to be associated only with religious education and acts of worship or with the whole curriculum. Those involved with CiE/CSC believed that it was essential that 'spiritual and moral' were interpreted as involving the whole of what was done in school and were not just seen as the 'output' of acts of worship and RE lessons. A particular problem that they faced resulted from earlier pressure from the Roman Catholic Church and the Church of England. These providers of voluntary and grant-maintained schools had insisted on, and been granted in the 1992 Act, the right for 'denominational education' to be inspected by someone specifically appointed by the foundation governors or governing body. Usually this meant that the 'denominational education' (the religious education given otherwise than in accordance with an agreed syllabus) was to be inspected by a representative of the denomination in question. In religious schools, the RE part of the basic curriculum was not to be inspected in the same way as the rest of the curriculum, but by people with knowledge of the denomination's faith and philosophy of education. Moreover, the person appointed need not be a registered inspector. As the Northbourne amendments were added to the 1992 Act at a late stage, their full impact was not immediately recognised. The churches came to believe that there was also a need for similar concessions concerning inspection of the Act of Worship and the general inspection of 'spiritual, moral, social and cultural development'. While those from CiE/CSC recognised the wisdom of this demand, in that secular and ill-informed inspectors could well give hostile inspection reports if they did not understand the school's basic philosophy, they were concerned that this move implied that 'spiritual and moral' could be separated from the rest of the school's work. As Deakin and Jones (193: 11) state,

> ...we must be very careful that we do not repeat the fatal mistake of 1839 (when the first HMIs were appointed). On no account must the neutrality of the secular curriculum be conceded. It is only too easy for references to spiritual and moral development/vales to be understood almost entirely as references to RE and collective worship. The only exception to this mind-set is the concession that value references *added* to the secular domains should be included, i.e., where attention is drawn to the 'inspirational' or 'uplifting' nature of works of art, literature or music or to the moral questions raised by humanities topics or in the applications of science and technology. The unstated assumption, of course, is that the essential core content of the secular subjects is value free. In contradiction to this, we must insist that all the secular curricula are framed within a cultural understanding; they are all moulded by a world-view... This world-view, these 'religious' 'values', should be placed openly on the table.

CiE/CSC thus became involved with others in trying to influence the way in which Ofsted's *Framework for the Inspection of Schools* developed. It is not possible to assess their precise influence, for there were several different groups trying to shape the *Framework*, but some interesting shifts in interpretation can be seen as the process progressed. In this process, it is highly likely that the individual personalities and beliefs of the new Secretary of State and the newly appointed Chief Inspector for Schools, Professor Stewart Sutherland, both had an impact. Stewart Sutherland was appointed as part-time Chief Inspector for Schools alongside his existing job as Vice Chancellor of the University of London. His family background in Scotland was one where religion had a strong influence, and he studied philosophy at Aberdeen University and philosophy of religion at Cambridge. He then taught in several universities before becoming Professor of History and Philosophy of Religion at King's College, London in 1977, Principal of the College in 1985, and Vice Chancellor of the University in 1990 (Holness, 1993). Such a person was unlikely to treat the problems of inspecting spiritual and moral values lightly. Indeed, he is reported to have been horrified by the idea of such inspection when the amendments were first accepted by Government.

Following early representations to the fledgling Ofsted, and knowing some of the background to the amendments, Sutherland requested a paper from CARE (CiE) setting out their ideas of how the assessment of values might be undertaken. Following a brainstorming session with CiE consultants a paper *Inspecting School Values* was produced and sent to the Chief Inspector in 1992 (Deakin, Marsh and Holt, 1992). The three authors were, respectively, the ex-Director of the Christian Schools Campaign, the Quality Manager of Avon TEC, and the Director of Christians in Education. The last, Anne Holt, also had considerable experience of politics and the Department of Education and Science for, besides her work at CiE, she advised the Department on governor training and for a time had an office in the Department.

It is not clear how much influence this document and associated lobbying had on the *Framework for Inspection*, but there are several differences in emphasis between the draft document sent out for consultation in mid 1992 and the final version dated August 1992. While both accept that pupils' spiritual and moral development concerns more than just the content of RE and collective worship, the first version (section 5.4, Ofsted, 1992a), has a much greater focus on RE and collective worship than does the revised version (section 5.3, Ofsted, 1992b). The revised version has a more extensive list of sources of evidence and

103

requirements that the report should include. It also uses the term 'whole curriculum' in its evaluation criteria statement.

The issue of spiritual and moral development has been the subject of continued discussion since this point. For example, the National Curriculum Council issued a brief discussion paper in April 1993, while the Office for Standards in Education produced a far more substantial discussion paper in February 1994. The latter makes it clear that, in their terms, 'spiritual development is a responsibility of the whole school and the whole of the curriculum, as well as the activities outside the curriculum' (Ofsted, 1994: 8). However, the debate is still not settled, for the March 1994 Framework revises the August 1993 Framework to provide a much watered-down version of the evaluation criteria. Where the 1993 version stated that,

> Spiritual development is to be judged by the extent to which pupils display:
>
> - a system of personal beliefs, which may include religious beliefs;
> - an ability to communicate their beliefs in discussion and through their behaviour;
> - willingness to reflect on experience and to search for meaning in that experience;
> - a sense of awe and wonder as they become more conscious of deeper meanings in the apparently familiar features of the natural world or in their experience,

the 1994 version was a more simple,

> Spiritual development is to be judged by how well the school promotes opportunities for pupils to reflect on aspects of their lives and the human condition through, for example, literature, music, art, science, religious education and collective worship, and how well the pupils respond.
>
> Inspectors should judge the extent to which the arrangements for acts of collective worship promote pupils' spiritual and other development.

This last formulation would appear to come close to falling into the trap of seeing most of the curriculum as secular and 'value free' as discussed by Deakin and Jones (1993) above. The Campaign's degree of success here is thus open to question.

The 1993 Education Act

John Patten, the new Secretary of State for Education in a newly restructured Department for Education, moved swiftly to produce a White Paper which was designed to increase 'Choice and Diversity' (DFE, 1992). It moved schooling one stage further down the path that Stuart Sexton had envisaged towards 'the supremacy of parental choice, the supremacy of purchasing power' (1987: 11), but it also tried to promote other more traditional values. The White Paper had one whole chapter devoted to spiritual and moral development, which John Patten claimed he had personally written. The chapter focused on four main issues: the importance of the school's role in promoting spiritual and moral development; the need for LEAs to review agreed syllabuses for religious education; the right of grant-maintained schools to teach any agreed syllabus for RE and not be restricted to that of their former LEA; and the right for grant-maintained schools to be involved in Standing Advisory Councils on RE. Some of what Patten wrote was particularly welcomed by those involved in CiE/CSC. For example, he stated forthrightly that,

> Education cannot and must not be value-free... At the heart of every school's educational and pastoral policy and practice should lie a set of shared values which is promoted in the curriculum, through expectations governing the behaviour of pupils and staff and through day to day contact between them (DFE, 1992: 37).

However, of greater importance for the wider campaign, the White Paper announced that the Government wished to see the creation of new schools and would be seeking to remove barriers to their creation:

> Patterns of schools that reflect the priorities of local authority planners, should be complemented or replaced by schools that reflect more widely the wishes and aspirations of parents. Growing diversity in education will be one of the features of the 1990s (DFE, 1992: 43).

By 1992, the New Right had moved into such an influential position and the ideology of choice was so powerful that it had become difficult to deny parents the right to set-up their own schools if they wished - they simply added to the diversity of schools which now were seen as a prerequisite for choice. In this respect the main features of the resulting 1993 Education Act were (see Walford, 1995c):

a. All secondary schools were given the right to 'specialise' in one or more curriculum areas such as science, music, technology or modern languages. All children are still required to follow the National Curriculum, but the 1992 White Paper and subsequent ministerial comment has encouraged the idea of extending the school day to make room for these specialisms. Further, the introduction of a specialism will not necessitate an official 'change of character' and schools are now allowed to select up to 10 per cent of their intake according to criteria related to the specialism.

b. The original White Paper encouraged an expansion of the idea of Technology Schools. These were said to build upon the work of the City Technology Colleges, and about 100 local authority, voluntary and grant-maintained schools received a total capital allocation of £25 million in 1992/93 to fund additional equipment and building improvements. This sum was increased in 1993/94, and a total of about 220 schools received funding over the two years. However, the scheme has now been discontinued and, in part, replaced by the Technology College initiative, which the White Paper envisaged as a parallel development.

c. The 1993 Education Act allowed voluntary aided and grant-maintained schools to apply to the Secretary of State for Education for a change to their governing Instruments and Articles such that up to four sponsor governors can be appointed to the governing body. This change allows such schools to become Technology Colleges - a modification to the City Technology College concept. The expectation is that grant-maintained or voluntary aided schools which already have a strong and planned commitment to technology, science and mathematics will be able to find sponsorship from industry in return for these seats on the governing body. The expectation is that there will be a 'significant financial commitment' from the sponsors (which was interpreted at the time of the announcement as being in the region of £100,000 per school), as well as close involvement by the sponsors in the life of the school. (This policy has since been extended to cover local authority schools as well.)

d. Finally, and crucially, the 1993 Education Act also encouraged diversification of schools through the establishment of new grant-maintained schools that support particular religious or philosophical beliefs. The Act gave powers to establish new grant-maintained school in two different ways. The first simply deals with cases where there is seen to be a need for a new school due to changes in population or similar circumstances, but the second allows sponsors to propose the establishment of new schools. Through this second procedure, the way is open for new Christian schools and other faith-based schools to be state funded. Existing faith-based private schools are now able to apply to become reestablished as grant-maintained schools.

This final point can be seen as marking the successful completion of the campaign initiated in 1988. These new sponsored grant-maintained schools will differ from existing grant-maintained schools in that sponsors will have to pay for at least 15 per cent of costs relating to the provision of a site for the school or school buildings. In return for this financial contribution, through the school's trust deeds and Instrument of Governance, the sponsors will be able to ensure that the school retains its original purpose. In particular, restrictions on making a 'significant change in the religious character' of these grant-maintained schools are explicitly built into the Act. Additionally, the sponsors will be able to appoint up to four sponsor governors onto the governing body. Some other foundation governors may be appointed by other people or bodies to be determined in the school's Instrument of Government, and the total of foundation governors must outweigh all other governors. In addition there must be two to five parent governors in the case of a primary school and five for a secondary school, one or two teachers and the Headteacher ex-officio. The composition of the governing body thus allows the sponsors to ensure that the religious objectives of the school are maintained and that the religious beliefs and practices of teaching staff are taken into consideration in appointments. The schools will have to teach the National Curriculum, but special arrangements for the teaching of religious education can detailed in the trust deed, and different arrangements are made concerning the character of collective religious worship. The admissions process can give preference to children from families with particular beliefs in the same way as existing Roman Catholic or Church of England voluntary schools.

While CiE/CSC were generally pleased with the developments outlined in the White Paper, there were several points that were unclear. CARE and CiE produced a 24-page analysis of the White Paper which covered a range of issues, including giving some attention to issues of possible inequity of funding for various schools. When the resulting Education Bill was published there remained areas that they felt needed further clarification. But for those who had been involved in the Christian Schools Campaign there were two major areas of concern. The first related back to the Northbourne amendments to the 1992 Education Act. While the major amendments had been successful, the Government had refused to put into primary legislation the need for schools to publish information on the values upon which it was intended that the spiritual, moral, social and cultural development of pupils in the school shall be based. It was stated at the time that Regulations would be drawn up to ensure that this occurred. However, by late 1992, this still had not been done. Michael Alison, MP, one of the active Christians involved with CARE, raised the issue in the second reading of the Bill on 9 November 1992, and was told by John Patten that he had instructed Ofsted to give great attention to such values in their reports and were 'setting great store by it' (Hansard, 9 November, 658). In Michael Alison's eyes Patten had 'made a fabulous contribution to the debate' with his short speech, and appeared content. CiE later attempted to introduce a new clause into the 1992 Education Bill/1993 Education Act which would have required the Secretary of State to issue Regulations setting out information to be published by schools on their values, but this motion was not introduced.

CiE/CSC's second remaining area of concern had more substance. The White Paper stated that:

> voluntary bodies will continue to be able to propose the establishment of new LEA maintained voluntary schools. In addition, once the 10 per cent entry point is reached, they will also be able to propose the establishment of new GM schools (DFE, 1992: 26).

This 10 per cent rule meant that it would not have been possible for new GM schools to have been established until there were already 10 per cent of primary or secondary pupils in an LEA's area already in GM schools. This corresponded to the 10 per cent point at which the Funding Agency takes on joint responsibility with the LEA for the provision of school places. But it was an arbitrary lower limit, and caused some consternation among some of the new Christian schools that hoped to take advantage of the new legislation.

Those who had been involved in the Christian Schools Campaign were central to amendments seeking to remove this ten per cent limit. Again, much of the political activity took place in the Lords and amendments were put by Lord Skidelsky and Baroness Cox to change the 10 per cent threshold. There was also considerable background lobbying such that, on 10 June 1993, Baroness Blatch announced that she had been persuaded by the arguments that the threshold was an unnecessary impediment and that a Government amendment would remove it. In her response to the announcement, Baroness Cox thanked Baroness Blatch for her acceptance of the change and said more about some of the schools that the change might effect.

> I know that a number of the new schools already set up by parents making great sacrifices - not the kind of parents who could normally pay independent school fees but those wanting a good education in areas where that was not necessarily available - would have fallen foul of the 10 per cent trip-wire. They will now be able to apply for grant-maintained status. For example, I was speaking today to the head of Oakhill school in Bristol, which is a new independent Christian school. It is an excellent school. [S]he said that the freeing of the 10 per cent trip-wire will enable that school to go ahead with an application. It would never otherwise have been able to do so. It will potentially save the life of that school if it is able to make a successful application (Lords Debates, Hansard, 10 June, 1993, cl. 1160).

Oak Hill School in Bristol is the school where Ruth Deakin, ex-Director of the Christian Schools Campaign, was formerly headteacher. As Avon had no GM schools at this point, a 10 per cent limit would have prohibited her school from applying. The change allowed Oak Hill to be one of the first schools to submit its application once the Funding Agency for Schools for England had been established in April 1994.

9 Part of a different agenda?

How is this account to be understood?

It would be relatively easy to interpret these important changes forced upon Government as an example of a pressure group's ability directly to influence legislation through the power of the arguments put forward. Such an interpretation might find support from those who believe in the rationality of our legislative processes, but other interpretations are possible and, indeed, more persuasive. There is little evidence that the outcomes of this sequence of pressure group activities can be more than partially understood through a rational decision-making model or, indeed, through models that give primacy to macro-economic or ideological variables. Instead, there is complexity where micropolitical negotiation, muddle and serendipity need to be understood within a wider macropolitical framework.

It is rarely possible to isolate the effects on public policy of the activities of one particular pressure group. While the 1993 Education Act does allow for state funding of faith-based schools through grant-maintained status, and this was the goal of the Christian Schools Campaign, such changes were also congruent with the wider aims of several other groups - especially those on the New Right. Nevertheless, the Campaign must be judged as having achieved its objectives, and there are particular instances (for example, changes in inspection criteria in the 1992 Act and the removal of the 10 per cent threshold in the 1993 Act) where the activities of those involved in the Campaign can be seen to have been highly influential.

This degree of success is remarkable, for the Campaign had only very limited funding and resources. For most of its existence, the Campaign was effectively one part-time unpaid Director with some very limited part-time support from the Steering Committee of six Headteachers of Christian schools. While, for a short period, the Campaign had some part-time secretarial and administrative support, most of the work on the Campaign was done by the Director alone.

Clearly there are several elements to the Campaign that helped in its success. Those establishing the Campaign already had links to highly active and successful political campaigners - in particular, Baroness Cox. They were encouraged and enabled to talk with Brian Griffiths, who was then Head of the Prime Minister's Policy Unit. There, they were given advice about how to create a campaign that might have influence. They were able to attract an impressive list of Patrons which increased the visibility of the campaign and gave publicity a better chance of being noticed, while the positions of the Patrons in the Lords and Commons meant that amendments to legislation could be put forward and debated. Further, the fact that the group was campaigning for *Christian* schools meant that the body of active Christians within both Houses were likely to give the Campaign their attention, if not support.

However, the fundamental reason for the Campaign's success must be that it fitted with various other and wider political agendas, in particular those of a section of the New Right. Parental choice has become a powerful ideological force which has been used, in part, to conceal the New Right's political objective for a more inequitable and hierarchical educational system. While, many of those on the New Right have made explicit their desire for a privatized educational system, based on individualistic choices, and on the ability and willingness of parents to pay, others have pushed for greater choice in the name of fairness. The Christian Schools Campaign became an important part of the pressure to achieve this long-term aim of a privatized system, and acted with others to influence Government such that this emphasis on individualistic choices became more acceptable. But, it was not simply that the objectives of the Christian Schools Campaign automatically fitted with those of Government or other pressure groups. In 1988, concerned about the potential extra costs, the Secretary of State was against new state funding for private schools. Similarly, only limited support for the idea was given by Government following Baroness Cox's Bill in 1991. In 1992, Ministers initially believed that it was not possible or desirable to inspect spiritual or moral development, but were forced to concede. It was only in 1992, with a new Secretary of State (who was also an active Roman Catholic) and after several years of campaigning, that the idea of support for a greater diversity of faith-based schools was officially allowed to surface.

Of course, it is not incidental that the preferred way of funding these new schools was through a new form of grant-maintained status. The number of LEA and voluntary schools choosing to become grant-maintained had been far lower than had been anticipated, with only 337 grant-maintained schools in operation by the beginning of 1993 (Fitz et al, 1993). These new schools would add to the total and make the policy appear more successful. The idea of making these new faith-based grant-maintained schools pay at least 15 per cent of the capital costs also fitted with plans for Technology Colleges which had developed from the City Technology Colleges and Technology Schools initiatives. Initially, for a school to become a Technology College it had to be grant-maintained or voluntary and the expectation was that there would be a 'significant financial commitment' from industrial sponsors (which was interpreted at the time of the announcement as being in the region of £100,000 per school), as well as close involvement by the sponsors in the life of the school. The idea of allowing existing private schools to become faith-based grant-maintained schools meshed with the idea of private sponsorship and finance becoming an integral part of the educational system.

Jenny Ozga (1990) warns us of the dangers of detailed studies of individual policies and policy-making processes that neglect to consider wider issues. She argues that such studies might provide rich descriptive data, but that they could also obscure the 'bigger picture' in trying to understand contemporary education policy. She strongly criticises approaches that generate 'a view of policy-making which stresses ad hocery, serendipity, muddle and negotiation' and which fail to set micro-political studies of personal relationships within a wider analysis of power. In contrast, Ball (1994: 14) takes issue with Ozga and argues that the complexity and scope of policy analysis preclude the possibility of single-theory explanations, and that what is needed is a more postmodern theoretical project of localized complexity. While accepting the clear need to 'bring together structural, macro-level analysis of educational systems and educational policies and micro-level investigation, especially that which takes account of people's perceptions and experience' (Ozga, 1990: 359), he claims that muddle, negotiation, and serendipity may be part of that micro-level activity. The challenge, as Ball (1994: 15) argues, is to 'relate together analytically the ad hocery of the macro with the ad hocery of the micro without losing sight of the systematic bases and effects of ad hoc social actions: to look for the iterations embedded within chaos.'

In many circumstances micropolitics can be used as a theoretical framework that avoids 'the reductionism associated with both holistic (structure) and individualistic (agency) frames of analysis (Troyna, 1994: 336). As Blase (1991: 1) indicates:

> Micropolitics is about power and how people use it to influence others and to protect themselves. It is about conflict and how people compete with each other to get what they want. It is about cooperation and how people build support among themselves to achieve their ends.

It is a framework with a strong commitment to try to link micro and macro theoretical concerns, and it recognises the constraints and possibilities of power at the macro level in its analysis.

This is well illustrated in the early stages of the work of the Christian Schools Trust. Here there are many examples of building support, forming alliances and taking advantage of the political resources of others. Baroness Cox's interest in evangelical Christian schools, and preexisting links with one of the schools was a crucial resource. As has been indicated earlier, Baroness Cox is one of a small group of right wing educationists whose ideas on education have gradually influenced government policy. She originally trained and practised as a nurse, then read sociology, and eventually became Head of the Sociology Department at the Polytechnic of North London. There she rose to prominence after publication of *The Rape of Reason* (1975) (coauthored with John Marks) which discussed student action within the Polytechnic of North London. From 1977 to 1984 she became Director of the Nursing Education Research Unit at Chelsea College, she was made Baroness in 1982, and from 1983 to 1985 was Director of the Centre for Policy Studies. She has been a key member of several small but influential right wing educational groups that have interlocking memberships, including the Hillgate Group which produced two influential pamphlets *Whose Schools?* (1986) and *The Reform of British Education* (1987). She is firmly in favour of selective schooling. For example, with John Marks and M. Pomian-Srzednicki, she examined the 1982 examination performance for over 2000 schools in 61 LEAs, and argued that the results showed a clear superiority for schools within a selective system over comprehensive schools (Marks et al, 1983). This research was the centre of a long dispute with the DES and with other researchers who claimed that the findings were erroneous (see, for example, Cox and Marks, 1988; Steedman, 1987; Preece, 1989). A later study by Marks and Pomian-Srzednicki (1985) found an advantage to the selective system in terms of average numbers of O levels and CSE grade 1 passes per pupil, but found no difference between the two systems when the full ability range was considered (Gray and Jesson, 1989). A balanced analysis of the several studies on this issue would indicate that, while the direction of difference is uncertain, the magnitude of differences is small. Nevertheless, *Whose Schools?* ignores a vast range of research literature and presents a picture of decline in standards due to comprehensivisation.

The main thrust of the two Hillgate pamphlets is a strident attack on local education authorities, some of which are seen as being responsible for 'corrupting the minds and souls of the young' through anti-sexist, anti-racist and anti-heterosexist initiatives. A strong 'back to basics' movement is encouraged in terms of curriculum, selective admissions policies advocated for popular schools and a greater diversity of schools receiving funding directly from central government is proposed. The second pamphlet makes it clear that the long term aim is that of a privatized education system with a 'pupil entitlement' or voucher from the government which would be encashable at fee-paying as well as non-fee-paying schools.

To attain this long-term aim Baroness Cox and others on the political right with similar aims (for example, Sir Rhodes Boyson and Stuart Sexton) have actively supported a variety of new small schools in the name of parental choice, and have claimed that the existence of these schools is an indicator of growing dissatisfaction with LEA provision. Diversity is encouraged, and opting out of LEA schools into schools that cater for idiosyncratic parental demands is presented as a positive response to the perceived shortcomings of the state system. This means that some of the schools that have received active support from the educational New Right have had some features with which they might actually disagree. For example, the standard of physical facilities available has sometimes been low, and styles and standards of teaching have varied widely. This contradiction is well illustrated in the case of the new Christian schools, some of which are in cramped buildings and offer poor facilities.

This initial contact with Baroness Cox was probably crucial to the Campaign, for it gave the group information and access. It enabled a small group of headteachers to meet with key decision-formers in Margaret Thatcher's Government, and within various educational pressure groups. Brian Griffiths (who then was Head of the Prime Minister's Policy Unit) not only listened to their objectives, but actively made suggestions on how they might best proceed politically. Some of these headteachers were subsequently introduced to other activists on the New Right or met them through attendance at regular meetings of Baroness Cox's Education Issues Group. This Educational Issues Group, which met irregularly in the House of Lords throughout the period, was concerned with a wide range of educational issues. It provided a platform for sharing of information between different New Right education groups and served as a meeting place for networking between activists. Stewart Sexton, for example, could be approached to draft a Private Member's Bill even though his interests are not primarily in Christian schools, but in working towards a more privatised system.

The Christian Schools Campaign can also be seen to have acted micropolitically in the way it constructed a list a Patrons that included members of all the major political parties. This activity was not a complete success. Many Bishops were approached by letter to try to gain their support, and the one who responded positively had a Bishop's Chaplain who was already a Patron himself. As it happened, this Bishop (George Carey) was subsequently translated to Canterbury, and felt it necessary to resign on recognising that there appeared to be a conflict of interest between his Patronage of the CSC and support of his own Church of England schools.

Alliances were made with other pressure groups pushing for similar changes to the law. An alliance with Human Scale Movement demanded little compromise, for many of their beliefs about education were very similar. In contrast, an alliance with various Muslim education groups caused more heart-searching. Some of the Christian schools involved were bitterly against the possibility of Muslim schools funded by the state. However, other wider political events such as the Gulf War and the Salman Rushdie *fatwa*, made it politically inappropriate for Muslim groups to continue to take a high profile, so this alliance weakened as the campaign progressed.

In each of these cases it is possible to see micro-level political interaction, networking, and the forming of strategic alliances. But it is also possible to see the influence of macro-structural power structures and ideologies along with Ball (1994) calls the muddle, ad hocery and serendipity of both micro- and macro-level activity. Some of the Christian Schools Campaign's objectives meshed with those of those of the New Right. Baroness Cox, Brian Griffiths and Stuart Sexton all wished to see a more market-led educational system. They were prepared to help because the aims of the Campaign fitted with their longer term objectives and with the Government's ideological thrust towards privatization and individualistic competition. But the exact fit between these various objectives was not always clear. The inspection of 'spiritual and moral' values, which was introduced through the Northbourne amendments, might fit well with the values of neo-conservative faction of the New Right, but had less appeal to the neo-liberal wing which emphasises individualism, free choice and the market. This particular legislative change might be thought of as serendipity in action, but a serendipity that was structured by wider patterns of power and control.

The Christian Schools Campaign was thus successful in achieving its aims, but those involved are not natural allies of the New Right. The new Christian schools became enmeshed within this wider political programme, because of their own individualistic desires to obtain funding for their own schools. But it is clear from research in the schools that many of those involved would not wish to be associated with any plans for an inequitable educational system. Indeed, the schools themselves often have fee policies that attempt to redress inequalities by charging according to ability to pay. Many try to offer open access, irrespective of ability to pay, and their curriculum is one which emphasises the Christian virtues of sharing and caring for others. In this case, there are considerable ironies in the success of the Christian Schools Campaign in obtaining the legislation for state funding of new Christian schools for this success had added to a potential for inequity which they would not support.

How many will apply?

The Christian Schools Campaign developed from the Christian Schools Trust, so it might be expected that many of the schools linked to the Trust will make application for grant-maintained status. Is the number of grant-maintained schools soon to be rapidly expanded by a host of new Christian schools?

Some information on this was gathered through the interview and postal survey of the schools with links to the Christian Schools Trust discussed in chapter two. The survey found that the schools ranged considerably in size from less than ten to nearly two hundred children, with a total of more than 3000 children in the 53 schools responding to the survey. Table 1, in chapter two, showed the distribution of size of school, and it was seen that most of the schools had less than 60 pupils, but that there was another substantial group of ten schools that had over 100 children. All except two of the schools had primary aged children. The two that did not were secondary schools linked with a separate primary school. About half of the schools catered for primary age children only, but the rest usually taught the full compulsory school age range up to 16.

When asked specifically if they thought that they might take advantage of the 1993 Education Act's proposals to allow new religious grant-maintained schools, only 30 per cent said they did, while 40 per cent replied in the negative. Others said that they did not have sufficient information, were undecided, or did not answer the question. Where schools were particularly small, a negative response may have been a reasonable assessment of their chances. About two-thirds of the schools had 60 or fewer pupils, and only 19 per cent of these schools thought they might apply for grant-maintained status. Forty-nine per cent of these smaller schools stated that they would not be applying. In practical terms, it is unrealistic to expect any schools with 60 or fewer pupils to have any chance of being given grant-maintained status by the Secretary of State. Most of these small schools use very simple accommodation (often church buildings) and rely on teachers who receive little or no pay. Moreover, they have few reserves of funding to be able to provide the required 15 per cent of the costs of new buildings.

Of the larger schools with over 60 pupils, 56 per cent (9 schools) stated that they might apply for grant-maintained status, 19 per cent (3 schools) stated that they would not be applying and 25 per cent (4 schools) did not answer. These results should be treated with some caution as several of the answers underlined the word 'might' in the question which asked whether they thought their school might take advantage of the possibility of applying for grant-maintained status. However, they give an indication of the maximum likely number of new Christian schools thinking about the possibility at that time. From other information, it was felt likely that only one of the few large schools which did not reply to the questionnaire might apply for grant-maintained status.

In the end, nine or ten of the survey schools linked to the Christian Schools Trust would seem to be large enough to have a reasonable chance of becoming grant-maintained and also might wish to do so. The Steering Committee for the Christian Schools Trust had a Director and six other members - representing seven schools in all. Six of these seven schools are among the seven largest schools that stated that they might consider grant-maintained status. All six had over 100 pupils each. Only three other schools with 60 or more pupils thought they might take advantage of the new opportunity, one of these had just over 60 pupils, one had just over 100 (but both figures include nursery) and one had about 150 pupils.

One of the schools with a representative on the Steering Committee for CSC closed in July 1993 due to financial problems, which gives eight or nine schools with over 60 pupils or seven or eight with over 100 pupils which might benefit. However, one or two of these make significant use of the packaged curriculum, Accelerated Christian Education (ACE), which was discussed in chapter two and has been the subject of considerable criticism from HMI. These schools are thus unlikely to be given grant-maintained status. Further, the numbers for the two smaller schools include nursery and thus have a lower number of children of school age than would be suggested. Others of the larger schools have continuing problems of finance and accommodation.

Assessing the overall responses, the most startling finding from the questionnaire and interview survey is that, in all, probably as few as five schools are reasonable candidates for the new grant-maintained school status. What is more, all these had representatives on the Steering Group for CSC. A small campaigning group has been able to successfully front a major change in educational policy, yet the vast majority of the group of schools it claimed to represent are unlikely to benefit. Indeed, as shown earlier, far from all of the schools in the group are active supporters of state funding. A few of the schools were resolutely against the Campaign's objectives, while others supported it only in terms of the 'righteousness' of the objectives.

This rather strange result could occur because the new Christian schools are very isolated from each other. Not only are they geographically spread, but there are theological differences between them that they were unwilling to address, but which eventually led to the demise of the Christian Schools Campaign itself. Further, for nearly all the schools, there were far more pressing concerns with survival and the everyday problems of running a school than those of campaigning for legal changes. As late as 1993, there was evidence from the interviews and questionnaires that many of the headteachers had not thought deeply about the implications of government funding. There was often a feeling that, as taxpayers, there was some right to get funding, and the individualistic argument that parents were currently 'paying twice' for education was routinely cited. But there was little evidence of a wider consideration of the issues in terms of equity or how the changes might be seen as part of right-wing plans for greater diversity of schooling within a competitive market environment.

Where there was evidence of deeper consideration of the implications of government funding for new Christian schools, there was often concern that other faith-based schools might also be able to obtain funding. A particular concern for some headteachers was that the campaign would make it easier for Muslim schools to obtain funding, which was generally seen as undesirable - if not against the will of God. Many of the schools definitely did not want government funding for their own schools for fear of the effects that such funding would have on the autonomy and mission of their schools. Some headteachers were also anxious about the methods used by the campaign to achieve its objectives, and specifically the way the campaign had worked with Muslims and with right-wing politicians whose aims might be very different from those of many of the schools. There was a recognition by a few that allowing faith-based schools to become grant-maintained might be part of a far wider right-wing plan for education which could have deeply undesirable results. The 1993 Education Act has made it possible for one or two new Christian schools to apply for grant-maintained status, but it might be argued that the success of the Christian Schools Campaign has brought a more diverse, competitive and inequitable system one stage nearer - an 'achievement' that many of the schools in the group would deeply regret.

10 Conclusion

Social and equity issues

The right to establish faith-based grant-maintained schools must be considered within the context of wider government and right-wing policy towards educational provision, for the Campaign was only successful because its aims could be encompassed within broader policy concerns. Under the mastheads of 'choice' and 'diversity', Government policy has been designed to increase the proportion of funding for schooling coming from the private sector, reintroduce selection, and legitimise inequity of provision for different groups of children (Walford, 1990a, 1994d). As many disillusioned parents have found, once popular schools are oversubscribed, it is the schools that select children rather than parents having a 'choice' of school. Within each area there is a likelihood that a hierarchy of schools will develop, and there is growing evidence that various privileged groups are better able than others to influence the selection of their children by those schools at the top of the hierarchy. Those with most concern about the education of their children are able to 'play the system' such that their children have a greater chance of being selected by the prestigious schools (Ball, 1993; Gewirtz et al, 1994). Moreover, the Government has shown little concern about the deleterious effects that increased diversity may have on equity and justice for all children, but appears to be content that those concerned and active parents who have the ability and means to influence the selection process can obtain their chosen schools. Faith-based grant-maintained schools certainly add to the diversity of schools available, but what are their implications in terms of equity and justice for all children?

In practice, the Christian Schools Campaign was seen by many of its supporters as centrally concerned with equity, justice and Christian 'righteousness'. It was argued that parents have the right to educate their children in the way they wish, especially in respect of religious beliefs, and that existing schools present a secular view of society that is in conflict with the views that parents hold and wish to transmit to their children. Moreover, in having to establish their own private schools to educate their children in the ways they wished, Christian parents, it was argued, are 'paying twice' for schooling - once through general taxation, and again by providing their own schools.

Such a view has considerable power for, in many ways, the right for Muslim, Hindu, and evangelical Christian parents to apply to have their own schools supported by the state might be seen as a gain in equity. Why should these parents feel forced to establish their own private schools (often at considerable financial sacrifice) to enable them to ensure that their children are educated according to their own wishes, while the Church of England, the Roman Catholic Church and some Jewish groups have their own state-funded schools? However, this interpretation of equity is essentially an individualistic view where parents seek what they believe to be best for their own children while ignoring or discounting the possible effect of their actions on others. It overlooks the possible effects on other people's children - both Christian and non-Christian.

A major consideration is that it is far from clear that society as a whole will benefit from some Muslim, Hindu or Christian children being educated separately from other children. In a pluralist and multi-ethnic country such as Britain, there is a need for children to mix with those of other faiths and ethnicities if they are to begin to understand, accept and enjoy each other's differences. It is almost inevitable that some faith-based grant-maintained schools will become segregated ethnically as well as religiously, which will do little to decrease racism and intolerance. One has only to look at the positive aspects of integrated schools in Northern Ireland to see the desirability of cultural and ethnic mixing as opposed to the problems of segregated schooling.

The establishment of some faith-based grant-maintained schools also has potential detrimental effects on those children of parents of that faith who remain within existing schools. It will only be possible to establish an evangelical Christian, Muslim or Hindu school in geographical areas where there are sufficient potential pupils to ensure the school's long term viability. There will always be many parents who do not have access to a faith-based school of their choice, and there will be others who do not wish their children to be in a segregated school yet still wish them to follow their religious faith. Both groups of parents may be disadvantaged by the existence of faith-based schools, for other schools may be less likely to take into account the needs of their children. Thus, for example, while several existing county and Church schools make arrangements for the regular worship demands of Islam and provide appropriate facilities, there may be less pressure on them to do so if the most vocal and forceful parents decide to place their children in a separate faith-based grant-maintained school.

An additional problem is that these new faith-based schools will bring a further form of selection and differentiation of children. Once the schools are oversubscribed, they will be forced to select, and the basis of selection may depend upon tests and interviews at which particular groups of parents and children will be likely to be successful and others more likely to fail. In particular, schools will be able to have admissions criteria that give preference to members the sponsoring group's faith (this can apply to the selection teachers as well as pupils). This may involve a simple affirmation or a test of active involvement with supporting evidence. Those families where education and faith are already valued will probably have an advantage over those where education is of little interest.

There is also a need to consider the balance that is to be made between the rights and responsibilities of parents and those of their children. The debate about choice in education has been dominated by the idea of 'parents' rights'. Yet democratic societies recognise that education is not purely the responsibility of parents. The state requires parents to 'cause their children to be educated' either by sending them to school or otherwise. Local education authorities are required to check that this is being done and to act on behalf of the child's and society's interests where it is not. In maintaining this requirement, society recognises that it is occasionally necessary to protect children from the wishes of their parents in matters of education as well as in health, welfare and safety.

For any school to be given grant-maintained status it would need to meet a variety of different criteria established by the Department for Education. However, the main demands are that the National Curriculum is followed, that there are adequate facilities and trained staff and that there are sufficient potential applicants to make the school viable. There is nothing in the requirements for grant-maintained status that determines the way that the National Curriculum should be taught or restricts (beyond wider race relations legislation) what additional material can be taught. Indeed, the new legislation clearly encourages parents to try to establish their own schools if their beliefs conflict with the teaching methods adopted in mainstream schools. Any group, whether it represents Jehovah's Witnesses, Exclusive Brethren, or mainstream Church of England, is treated equally. There is nothing in the legislation that prohibits fundamentalist followers of any religion proposing their own grant-maintained schools where authoritarian obedience to the faith and its ordained practices are inculcated.

This is not the place to enter the wider philosophical debate about the nature of education and knowledge. My own position follows the liberal position of Pring (1992), Bailey (1984) and many others in believing that education is centrally concerned with activities that draw upon 'a specific critical tradition which enables facts to be challenged and informed argument to be engaged in' (Pring, 1992: 25), and that there needs to be a balance between failing to respect differences of value and aspiration of distinct groups within our society and accepting that all values and beliefs are equally acceptable irrespective of their anti-democratic and miseducative results.

In this context, some features of the teaching within the new Christian schools are of concern. Of the 53 new Christian schools responding to the survey (Poyntz and Walford, 1994), all but one taught Biblical creation as fact. Two-thirds of the schools taught evolution as well as creation, but all of them treated it as a theory in contrast to the 'factual' nature of the creation story. In nearly all cases it was taken for granted that the Bible's account of six day creation was literally true, and the evolutionary view was false. Two typical responses were:

We present the facts to the children, and it's obvious what's right and what's wrong.

[Evolution is taught] Only as a discredited theory..... children have to know why so many books, programmes, etc. say such things as dinosaurs lived millions of years before man 'evolved'.

This dogmatism was also reflected in the schools' attitudes towards other faiths and in questions of morality. Several of the schools took care to 'edit' well-known reading books for younger children, while others chose GCSE English boards on the basis of the moral stance of the novels students were asked to read. While there was variation between the schools, and some were more open to debate between conflicting opinions, in several schools the degree of indoctrination was high. Such examples suggest that the current legislation may not have given sufficient consideration to the balance between the rights and responsibilities of parents and those of their children.

Conclusion

The idea that the state should fund a variety of different schools according to parents' wishes has a powerful simplicity which has welded together a remarkable range of people and organizations from the political right and left. Freedom of choice has become a powerful ideological force - but it is one that has been used to partly conceal the right's political objective of a more individualistic and inequitable educational system. The proponents of faith-based grant-maintained schools reflect this individualistic orientation. But, while it is perfectly right and proper that parents should wish to make choices on behalf of their children for their perceived benefit, their decisions are not always correct, and what is good for the individual is not always good for society as a whole or for certain less privileged groups within that society. Individual choices, and the sum effect of individual choices, may have benefits for those making choices, but may also harm others who are less able or willing to participate in the choice-making process (Walford, 1994a). The presence of faith-based schools, for example, may harm those children from the same faith who remain in state schools by taking out from the state sector those parents who are most likely to ensure that appropriate provision and teaching are maintained. The education provided in state schools may thus deteriorate with the exit of those parents with the greatest concern for their faith. Children of minority faith, majority faith or no faith at all could all be disadvantaged. Moreover, it is the duty of the state to ensure that one group of children is not harmed by the actions of the others - a duty which may mean that individual freedoms are constrained for the benefit of the society as a whole.

The solution is not straightforward, for there needs to be a balance between the desires of individuals and society's need to ensure that schools do not become elitist or segregationist. The Christian schools are not themselves elitist. Some of them currently serve children from the most deserving segments of our society, and most of them are prepared to accept a small number of non-Christian children where they have room. Furthermore, the schools have good grounds for asking for state support, as some 22 per cent of children in state maintained schools are already in religious denominational schools. The most equitable and socially beneficial solution would be to discontinue voluntary aided and grant-maintained status and encourage all schools to adapt to and encourage the faiths of its pupils. Such a solution is not a political possibility. Thus, in the interests of equity, it is necessary to allow other voluntary bodies to have a major influence in state-maintained schools. The most appropriate way of doing this is through the LEAs (or some similar locally democratic bodies (National Commission on Education, 1993)) rather than by any new type of grant-maintained or voluntary school. To prevent schools becoming elitist or segregationist these new schools should be under the general supervision of the LEAs, and should work in cooperation with other schools. They should have their own ethos and cover such additional curriculum areas as they see fit beyond the National Curriculum. LEAs would act to monitor and maintain standards and to ensure that no religious, ethnic or cultural entry conditions were imposed. They would also have the responsibility to ensure that schools made no attempt to indoctrinate children with particular beliefs, but encouraged a balanced debate on faiths and faith-related activities. Such conditions would be too strict for some of the new Christian and Muslim schools to accept, but they are necessary if an equitable education system is to be available to all children.

Bibliography

Advisory Centre for Education (1979) *A Case for Alternative Schools within the Maintained Sector* (London, ACE)

Alison, M. and Edwards, D.L. (1990) (eds.) *Christianity and Conservatism* (London, Hodder & Stoughton)

Apple, M.W. (1981) 'Curriculum control and the logic of curriculum control.' In L.Barton, R.Meighan and S.Walker (eds.) *Schooling, Ideology and the Curriculum* (London, Falmer)

Apple, M.W. (1982) *Education and Power* (London, Routledge & Kegan Paul)

Apple, M.W. (1987) *Teachers and Texts* (London, Routledge & Kegan Paul)

Bailey, C. (1984) *Beyond the Present and the Particular: A theory of liberal education* (London, Routledge & Legan Paul)

Ball, S.J. (1987) *The Micro-Politics of the School* (London, Methuen)

Ball, S.J. (1990a) *Politics and Policy Making in Education* (London, Routledge)

Ball, S.J. (1990b) *Markets, Morality and Equality in Education* Hillcole Group Paper 5 (London, The Tufnell Press)

Ball, S. (1993) 'Education markets, choice and social class: the market as a class strategy in the UK and the USA' *British Journal of Sociology of Education*, 14, 1, pp. 3-19.

Ball, S.J. (1994) *Educational Reform. A critical and post-structural approach* (London, Routledge)

Baxter, T. (1991) *Schould Christian Schools Seek State or Public Funding?* (Whitby, Foundation for Christian Reconstruction)

Bell, L. (1989) 'Ambiguity models and secondary schools: A case study.' In Tony Bush (ed.) *Managing Education: Theory and Practice* (Buckingham,

Open University Press)

Berg, L. (1968) *Risinghill: Death of a Comprehensive School* (Harmondsworth, Penguin)

Blackburne, L. (1989) 'Thirty-one cooks plus a seasoned campaigner' *Times Educational Supplement* 10 March.

Blase, J. (1991) 'The micropolitical perspective.' In Joseph Blase (ed.) *The Politics of Life in Schools* (London, Sage)

Boyson, R. (1974) *Oversubscribed. The Story of Highbury Grove School* (London, Ward Lock)

Bush, T. (1994) 'Theory and practice in educational management.' In Tony Bush and John West-Burnham (eds.) *The Principles of Educational Management* (London, Longman)

Buswell, C. (1980) 'Pedagogic change and social change' *British Journal of Sociology of Education*, Vol. 1, no. 3, pp. 293-306.

Christian Parent-Teacher League (1981) Newsletter March.

Christian Schools Campaigns (1989) Information sheet April.

Christian Schools Trust (1988) Information sheet.

Clouser, R.A. (1991) *The Myth of Religious Neutrality* (London, University of Notre Dame Press)

Cohen, M.D. and March, J.G. (1974) *Leadership and Ambiguity: The American College President* 2nd edition (Harvard, MA, Carnegie Foundation for the Advancement of Training)

Cohen, M.D., March, J.G. and Olsen, J.P. (1972) 'A garbage can model of organizational choice' *Administrative Science Quarterly* 17, 1, pp. 1-25.

Cookson, P.W. Jr. (1989) 'United States of America: Contours of continuity and controversy in private schools.' In G.Walford (ed.) *Private Schools in Ten Countries:Policy and Practice* (London, Routledge)

Cox, C.and Marks, J. (1988) *The Insolence of Office* (London, The Claridge Press)

Cox, C., Jacka, K. and Marks, J. (1975) *The Rape of Reason* (London, Churchill Press)

Cox, C., Jacka, K.and Marks, J. (1977) 'Marxism, knowledge and the academies.' In C. B. Cox and R. Boyson (eds) *Black Paper 1977* (London, Temple-Smith)

Cox, C. B. and Dyson, A. (1971) (eds.) *The Black Papers on Education 1 - 3* (London, Davis-Poynter)

Cox, C. B. and Boyson, R. (1975) (eds.) *The Fight for Education. Black Paper*

1975 (London, Dent)

Cummings, D.B. (1979) *The Purpose of Christ-Centred Education* (Phillipsburg, New Jersey, Presbyterian and Reformed Publishing)

Deakin, R. (1989a) *The Case for Public Funding* (Bristol, Regius)

Deakin, R. (1989b) *The New Christian Schools* (Bristol, Regius)

Deakin, R. and Jones, A. (1993) *Towards Effective Christian Politics* (Bristol, Oak Hill School)

Demaine, J. (1993) 'The New Right and the self-managing school.' In Smyth, J. (ed.) *A Socially Critical View of the Self-Managing School* (London, Falmer)

Dennett, S. (1988) *A Case for Christian Education* (Bradford, Harvestime)

Department of Education and Science (1985a) *Report by HM Inspectors on New Court Christian School, Finsbury Park,London.* 176/85 (DES, London)

Department of Education and Science (1995b) *Education for All* (The Swann Report) (London, HMSO)

Department for Education (1992) *Choice and Diversity. A New Framework for Schools*, Cmnd 2021, July (London, HMSO)

Diamond, L. (1989) 'Building on the failure of CSSAS.' In C. Harber & R. Meighan (eds.) *The Democratic School* (Ticknall, Education Now)

Dooley, P. (1991) 'Muslim private schools.' In G. Walford (ed.) *Private Schooling: tradition, change and diversity* (London, Paul Chapman)

Doyle, D.P. (1989) 'Family choice in education: the case of Denmark, Holland and Australia.' In Boyd, W.L. and Cibulka, J.G. (eds.) *Private Schools and Public Policy* (London, Falmer)

Durham, M. (1991) *Sex and Politics. The family and morality in the Thatcher years* (London, Macmillan)

Dwyer, C. (1993) 'Constructions of Muslim identity and the contestation of power: the debate over Muslim schools in the United Kingdom.' In P. Jackson and J. Penrose (eds.) *Constructions of Race, Place and Nation* (London, UCL Press)

Enderud, H.G. (1977) *New Faces of Leadership in the Academic Organization* (Nyt Nordisk Foriag Arnold Busck, Copenhagen)

Fitz, J., Halpin, D. & Power, S. (1993) *Grant Maintained Schools* (London, Kogan Page)

Gewirtz, S., Ball, S. and Bowe, R. (1994) 'Parents, privilege and the educational market place' *Research Papers in Education*, 9, 1, pp. 3-29.

Golby, M., Treharne, D. and Taylor, W. (1989) *The Small School at Hartland:*

An evaluation (Tiverton, Fair Way Publications)

Gordon, T. (1986) *Democracy in One School?* (London, Falmer)

Gray, J and Jesson, D. (1989) 'The impact of comprehensive reforms.' In R. Lowe (ed.) *The Changing Secondary School* (London, Falmer)

Griffiths, B. (1990) 'The Conservative quadrilateral.' In M. Alison & D. L. Edwards (eds.) *Christianity and Conservatism* (London, Hodder & Stoughton)

Griggs, C. (1989) 'The new right and English secondary education.' In R. Lowe (ed.) *The Changing Secondary School* (London,Falmer)

Hackett, G. (1990) 'Parents "should get DES grants to set up schools"' *Times Educational Supplement* 29/6/90.

Halstead, M. (1991) 'Radical feminism, Islam and the single sex school debate' *Gender and Education* 3, 3, pp. 263-278.

Hargreaves, D.H. (1974) 'Deschoolers and the new romantics.' In Flude, M. and Ahier, J. (eds.) *Educability, Schools and Ideology* (Beckenham, Croom Helm)

Hillgate Group (1986) *Whose Schools?* (London, Hillgate Group)

Hillgate Group (1987) *The Reform of British Education* (London, The Claridge Press)

Holness, M. (1993) 'The philosopher king and the starry heavens above' *Church Times*, 17 September, p. 7.

Holt, A. (1993) 'Christians in education' *The Christian Schools Trust Newsletter*, Number 11, July, p.2.

Independent Schools Information Service (1995) *Annual Census* (London, ISIS)

Khanum, S. (1992) 'Education and the Muslim girl.' In Sahgal, G. & Yuval-Davis, N. (eds.) *Refusing Holy Orders* (London,Virago)

Lester, A. and Pannick, D. (1987) *Independent Schools. The Legal Case* (London, Independent Schools Information Service)

Lodge, B. (1990) 'Veto could cost votes, warns Musim leader' *Times Educational Supplement* 8/6/90.

Lodge, B. (1991a) 'Bishops oppose Christian grant bid' *Times Educational Supplement* 18/1/91.

Lodge, B. (1991b) 'Dr Carey turns on his own campaign' *Times Educational Supplement* 20 September.

Mackenzie, R F (1970) *State School* (Harmondsworth, Penguin)

Maitland, S. (1992) 'Biblicism: A radical rhetoric?' In Gita Sahgal and Nira Yuval-Davis (eds.) Refusing Holy Orders (London, Virago)

Marks, J. and Pomian-Srzednicki, M. (1985) *Standards in English Schools:*

Second Report (London, Sherwood Press)

Marks, J., Cox, C. & Pomian-Srzednicki, M. (1983) *Standards in English Schools* (London, National Council for Educational Standards)

Mason, P.(1989) 'Elitism and patterns of independent education.' In W.L. Boyd and J.G Cibulka (eds.) *Private Schools and Public Policy* (Lewes, Falmer)

Meighan, R. (1988) *Flexi-schooling* (Ticknall, Education Now)

Muslim Educational Trust (1992) *Comments on the Government White Paper Choice and Diversity. A new framework for schools* (London, Muslim Educational Trust)

Muslim Parliament of Great Britain (1992) *White Paper of Muslim Educatin in Great Britain* (London, Muslim Parliament of Great Britain)

National Commission on Education (1993) *Learning to Succeed* (London, Heinemann)

National Curriculum Council (1993) *Spiritual and Moral Development - A discussion Paper* (York, NCC)

Office for Standards in Education (1992a) *Framework for the Inspection of Schools. Paper for consultation* (London, Ofsted)

Office for Standards in Education (1992a) *Framework for the Inspection of Schools* (London, Ofsted)

Office for Standards in Education (1994) *Spiritual, Moral, Social and Cultural Development. An Ofsted discussion paper* (London, Ofsted)

O'Keeffe, B. (1986) *Faith, Culture and the Dual System* (Lewes, Falmer)

O'Keeffe, B. (1992) 'A look at the Christian schools movement.' In B. Watson (ed.) *Priorities in Religious Education* (London, Falmer)

Ozga, J. (1990) 'Policy research and policy theory: a comment on Fitz and Halpin' *Journal of Education Policy*, 5, 4, pp. 359-362.

Peshkin, A. (1986) *God's Choice. The Total World of a Fundamentalist Christian School* (Chicago, Chicago University Press.

Pirie , M, (1992) *The Radical Edge* (London, Adam Smith Institute)

Poyntz, C. & Walford, G. (1994) 'The new Christian schools: A survey' *Educational Studies* 20, 1, 127-143.

Preece, P. (1989) 'Pitfalls in research on school and teacher effectiveness' *Research Papers in Education*, Vol. 4, no. 3, pp. 47-69.

Pring, R. (1992) 'Education for a pluralist society.' In L. Leicester and M. Taylor (eds.) *Ethics, Ethnicity and Education* (London, Kogan Page)

Pyke, N. (1995) 'Muslims vow to try again' *Times Educational Supplement* 24/2/95, p. 11.

Rae, J. (1981) *The Public School Revolution* (London, Faber)

Rose, S. D. (1988) *Keeping them out of the Hands of Satan. Evangelical Schooling in America* (London, Routledge & Kegan Paul)

Sahgal, G. & Yuval-Davis, N. (eds.) *Refusing Holy Orders* (London, Virago)

Sexton, S. (1987) *Our Schools - A Radical Policy* (Warlingham, Surrey, Institute for Economic Affairs Education Unit)

Sexton, S. (1992) *Our Schools - Future Policy* (Warlingham, Surrey, IPSET Education Unit)

Skinner, G.B. (1981) *Faith and Education: Some alternative models.* Unpublished DASE dissertation, University of Manchester.

Steedman, J.(1987) 'Longitudinal survey results into progress in secondary schools, based on the National Child Development Study.' In G. Walford (ed.) *Doing Sociology of Education* (Lewes, Falmer)

Toogood, P. (1988) 'Painting a cage with the cage door open' *Education Now*, no. 1, pp. 16-17.

Toogood, P. (1989) 'Learning to own knowledge: Minischools as democratic practice.' In C. Harber and R. Meighan (eds) *The Democratic School* (Ticknall, Education Now Publishing)

Troyna, B. (1994) 'The "everyday world" of teachers? Deracialised discourses in the sociology of teachers and the teaching profession' *British Journal of Sociology of Education*, 15, 3, pp. 325-339.

Van Brummelen, H. (1988) *Walking with God in the Classroom* (Burlington, Ontario, Welch Publishing)

Walford, G. (1990a) *Privatization and Privilege in Education* (London, Routledge)

Walford, G. (1990b) 'Developing choice in British education' *Compare*, Vol. 20, no. 1, pp. 67-81.

Walford, G. (1991) 'The reluctant private sector: Of small schools, politics and people.' In G. Walford (ed.) *Private Schooling: tradition, change and diversity* (London, Paul Chapman)

Walford, G. (1993) (ed.) *The Private Schooling of Girls: Past and present* (London, Woburn Press)

Walford, G. (1994a) *Choice and Equity in Education* (London, Cassell)

Walford, G. (1994b) 'Weak choice, strong choice and the new Christian schools.' In J. M. Halstead (ed.) *Parental Choice and Education* (London, Kogan Page)

Walford, G. (1994c) 'The new religious grant-maintained schools' *Educational*

Management and Administration, 22, 2, pp. 123 - 130.

Walford, G. (1994d) 'A return to selection?' *Westminster Studies in Education*, 17, pp. 19-30.

Walford, G. (1995a) 'The Northbourne amendments: Is the House of Lords a garbage can?' *Journal of Education Policy*, 10, 4.

Walford, G. (1995b) 'Faith-based grant-maintained schools: selective international policy borrowing from the Netherlands' *Journal of Education Policy*, 10, 3.

Walford, G. (1995c) 'Faith-based schools, diversity and inequity.' In G. Wallace (ed.) *Schools, Markets and Management* (Bournmouth, Hyde Publications)

Walford, G. & Miller, H. (1991) *City Technology College* (Buckingham, Open University Press)

Watts, J. (1980) *Towards and Open school* (London, Longman)

Whitcomb, L and Williams, N. (1993) *Stand Up and be Counted* (Eastbourne, Kingsway)

Whitty, G., Edwards, T. and Gewirtz, S. (1993) *Specialisation and Choice in Urban Education. The City Technology College experiment* (London, Routledge)

Winsor, D. (1987) 'Small is Educational' *Sunday Times Colour Supplement*, 4 October.

Wright, N. (1989) *Assessing Radical Education* (Milton Keynes, Open University Press)

Young, M. (1958) *The Rise of the Meritocracy* (Harmondsworth, Penguin)

Young, M. (1982) *The Elmhirsts of Dartington* (London, Routledge & Kegan Paul)

Young, M. and Willmott, P. (1957) *Family and Kinship in East London* (Harmondsworth, Penguin)

Young, M. and Willmott, P. (1973) *The Symmetrical Family* (London, Routledge & Kegan Paul)

Young, M. and Schuller, T. (1988) (eds.) *Rhythms of Society* (London, Routledge)

Index

About the author

Geoffrey Walford is course leader of the MSc Educational Research Methodology course and lecturer in educational studies in the Department of Educational Studies, University of Oxford, and a Fellow of Green College, Oxford. He was previously Senior Lecturer in Sociology and Education Policy at Aston Business School, Aston University, Birmingham. He has received academic degrees from Oxford, Kent, London and the Open Universities, and is author of more than 80 academic articles and book chapters. He is also author or editor of 15 books which include: *Life in Public Schools* (Methuen, 1986), *Restructuring Universities: Politics and power in the management of change* (Croom Helm, 1987), *Privatization and Privilege in Education* (Routledge, 1990) *City Technology College* (Open University Press, 1991)(with Henry Miller), *Choice and Equity in Education* (Cassell, 1994) and *Researching the Powerful in Education* (UCL Press, editor, 1994). His research into faith-based grant-maintained schools continues.

About the book

The 1993 Education Act opened the way for new grant-maintained schools to be established which support particular religious or philosophical beliefs. It enables existing private faith-based schools to 'opt in' to the state maintained sector. This change marks a fundamental shift in government policy towards religious schools and is the result of sustained activity by a small number of political pressure groups.

This book gives an account of that political activity, and focuses on the role of the Christian Schools Campaign which was responsible for significant changes in the 1992 and 1993 Education Acts. The Campaign, which represented about 65 small private evangelical Christian schools, has acted with other religious groups and politicians on the New Right to sponsor various amendments to government legislation.

This book describes the nature of the evangelical Christian schools in this group, and discusses the theological and pragmatic justifications used by parents and church groups in establishing and maintaining these separate schools. It presents a case-study of the activities of the Christian Schools Campaign, and a theoretical analysis which focuses on the nature of micropolitical activity by pressure groups. The analysis is set within the wider context of the policies of various New Right groups and shows the importance of the relationship between this pressure group's objectives and wider social and economic forces. Finally, the equity issues related to such a change in policy are examined.